# A Momentous Year in the Supreme Court

## OCTOBER TERM
## —2021—

ERWIN CHEMERINSKY

ABA
AMERICAN BAR ASSOCIATION
Judicial Division

Cover design by Amanda Fry/ABA Design
Interior design by Betsy Kulak/ABA Design



Printed in the United States of America.

26 25 24 23 22    5 4 3 2 1

ISBN: 978-1-63905-232-5
e-ISBN: 978-1-63905-233-2

*For my grandchildren,*
*Andrew, Sarah, and Amy*

# Contents

# Preface

For the second year in a row, I feel fortunate to have the opportunity to write this book for the American Bar Association summarizing the just-completed Supreme Court term. And as is reflected in the title and theme of this book, it was an especially momentous year in the Supreme Court.

These books are a result of a suggestion from Bob Edmunds and Herbert Dixon that I provide a written description of the term similar to the talks that I have been giving to judges and lawyers for more than 35 years. My goal, as in my talks, is to present the cases as clearly as I can and to explain their implications. My hope is to do this in a neutral manner, without evaluating them or editorializing. I certainly have views about many of them and cannot pretend that they do not sometimes affect my presentation of the cases. That is especially true about many of the cases this term—about topics like abortion, gun rights, separation of church and state. But my goal is to present the cases as fairly as I can and leave my normative judgments to be expressed in other places.

I want to express my great appreciation to my research assistants—Cameron Brown, Bailey Bryant, and Lawrence Myung—for their terrific assistance. And as always, my wonderful assistant, Whitney Mello, was invaluable. Catherine Fisk and Alex Chemerinsky talked through many of the ideas in the book and, as always, their insights were enormously helpful.

1

# Introduction

The Supreme Court's October 2021 Term was one of the most momentous in history. The only analogy I can think of is 1937 for its dramatic changes in constitutional law. In two decisions, on March 29 and April 12, 1937, the Supreme Court overruled 40 years of precedents that had declared unconstitutional federal and state laws protecting workers and consumers. I believe that October Term 2021 will be regarded as similarly dramatic in the way that it changed constitutional law. This was the first full term with Justice Amy Coney Barrett on the Court, and we saw the enormous effects of having a 6–3 conservative majority. And it is a conservative majority that is likely to remain for years to come.

Before examining the cases in detail in the following chapters, this introduction provides an overview of the term. Also, this term saw the retirement of Justice Stephen Breyer and the confirmation of Justice Ketanji Brown Jackson. What is that likely to mean for the Court?

## October Term 2021 by the Numbers

In October Term 2021, the Court decided 60 cases after briefing and oral argument. That is slightly more than the 53 rulings and the 54 rulings from the prior two years, but still significantly less than it used to be. In the 1980s, the Court often decided over 150 cases a year. In Chief Justice William Rehnquist's last year, the October Term 2004, the Court decided 85 cases.

Of the 60 cases, 19 were decided 6–3, and nine were decided by a 5–4 margin. Only 29 percent were unanimous, the smallest in recent memory. Chief Justice John Roberts and Justice Brett Kavanaugh were most often in the majority, in 95 percent of the cases. Justice Sonia Sotomayor was least often in the majority, in just 58 percent of the decisions.

## How Did We Get Here?

It is important at the outset, before reviewing cases of the term, to consider how we came to have this Court. From 1960 to 2020, there were 32 years with a Republican president and 28 years with a Democratic president. Although this is almost exactly even (and will be even in 2024), during this time, Republican presidents picked 15 justices, and Democratic presidents selected only eight justices. Put another way: President Donald Trump chose three Supreme Court justices in four years in office. By contrast, the last three Democratic presidents—Jimmy Carter, Bill Clinton, and Barack Obama—served a combined 20 years in the White House and, during that time, appointed only four justices.

Some of this reflects the accident of timing for when vacancies occurred. President Richard Nixon picked four justices in his first two years in office, while President Jimmy Carter had no vacancies on the Court in his four years in the White House. But the Court's composition also reflects Senate Majority Leader Mitch McConnell successfully blocking consideration of President Obama's nomination of Chief Judge Merrick Garland to replace Justice Antonin Scalia. McConnell also successfully rushed through the confirmation of Justice Amy Coney Barrett, who was approved by the Senate just a week before the November 2020 election.

The importance of the election of Donald Trump for the composition of the Court cannot be overstated. President Trump's three nominees—Neil Gorsuch, Brett Kavanaugh, and Amy Coney Barrett—were in the majority in every major conservative ruling. The simple reality is that if Hillary Clinton had been elected in 2016, none of the major cases would have come out the same way.

## Moving the Law Dramatically in a Conservative Direction

The numbers recited above about the term do not tell the full story. The most important theme of October 2021 is that virtually every major case was resolved in a conservative direction. According to an analysis by the *New York Times*, this was the most conservative term since 1931.[1] The Court's rulings were on some of the most divisive issues in American society, and in each, the Court divided ideologically and moved the law sharply to the right. The cases are presented and discussed in detail in the subsequent chapters of this book, but the dramatic conservative turn of the Court is reflected specially in a few high-profile decisions:

**Abortion.** This Term will be most remembered for the ruling on June 24, 2022, in *Dobbs v. Jackson Women's Health Organization*.[2] The Supreme Court overruled *Roe v. Wade* and held that no longer does the Constitution protect a woman's right to abortion prior to viability. The Court said that *Roe v. Wade* was "egregiously wrong" and "exceedingly poorly reasoned." The issue of abortion is now left to the political process, with each state able to decide for itself whether to allow abortions or prohibit some or all abortions. But it also must be remembered that Congress could adopt a law creating a national right to abortion or forbidding all abortions, thus preempting state laws to the contrary.

**Religion.** In two decisions, the Court strongly protected free exercise of religion, but gave little, if any, weight to the Establishment Clause of the First Amendment. *Carson v. Makin* involved a Maine law that applies in areas that are too rural to support public school systems.[3] In these areas, school administrative units provide funds for parents to send their children to private schools. Maine requires that the money be used in secular, not "sectarian" schools. The Supreme Court, in a 6–3 decision split along ideological lines, ruled in favor of the challengers and concluded that Maine violated free exercise of religion in not subsidizing religious school education. Chief Justice Roberts wrote the opinion for the Court and held that whenever the government financially supports secular private schools, it is constitutionally required to subsidize religious education.

The other case about religion was *Kennedy v. Bremerton School District*,[4] involving Joseph Kennedy, a football coach at a public school in Bremerton, Washington. Although there was significant disagreement between the majority and the dissent over the facts, at the very least, both agreed that after games, Kennedy, a self-described devout Christian, would kneel at the 50-yard line and engage in prayer for about 30 seconds. At times, students and others would join him. The school system suspended him for this behavior. The Supreme Court, in another 6–3 decision, ruled that Kennedy's constitutional rights to free exercise of religion and freedom of speech were violated by keeping him from engaging in silent prayers on the football field after games. The Court thus not only said that the prayer was allowed, but that the school was required to permit it.

**Administrative Law.** The most important decision about administrative law came down on the last day of the term in *West Virginia v. Environmental Protection Agency*, which involves the authority of the EPA to regulate power plants to limit their greenhouse gas emissions from coal-fired power plants.[5] In a 6–3 decision, the Court held that the EPA was limited in regulating greenhouse gas emissions from power plants because Congress had not been sufficiently specific in granting this power in the Clean Air Act. The Court said that the authority to regulate greenhouse gas emissions from power plants is a "major question" and that when there is a major question, there must be explicit statutory provisions giving the federal agency the power to act. Chief Justice John Roberts, writing for the Court, declared that "something more than a merely plausible textual basis for the agency action is necessary. The agency instead must point to 'clear congressional authorization' for the power it claims."[6] This will lead to challenges to many agency actions on the ground that they concern a major question and Congress did not provide sufficiently specific guidance.

**Second Amendment.** *New York State Rifle and Pistol Association v. Bruen* involves a New York law, initially adopted in 1911, prohibiting having weapons in public without a permit.[7] If a person wants to carry a firearm outside the home or a place of business for self-defense, the applicant must obtain an unrestricted license to "have and carry" a concealed "pistol or revolver." To secure that license, the applicant must prove that "proper cause exists" to issue it. New York courts have interpreted this to require that a person "demonstrate a special need for self-protection distinguishable from that of the general community."

In a 6–3 decision, with the majority opinion written by Justice Clarence Thomas, the Court declared the New York law unconstitutional. The Court was explicit that "the Second and Fourteenth Amendments protect an individual's right to carry a hand-gun for self-defense outside the home."[8] The Court held that state laws are unconstitutional if they restrict having concealed weapons to those who show cause.

## The Emphasis on History

In these and other cases, the Court said that the meaning of a constitutional provision is determined by the historical understanding and practices when it was adopted. The term was a triumph for originalism, the view that the meaning of a constitutional provision is fixed when it is adopted and can be changed only by amendment. For example, in striking down the New York gun law, the Court declared:

> *To justify its regulation, the government may not simply posit that the regulation promotes an important interest. Rather, the government must demonstrate that the regulation is consistent with this Nation's historical tradition of firearm regulation. Only if a firearm regulation is consistent with this Nation's historical tradition may a court conclude that the individual's conduct falls outside the Second Amendment's "unqualified command."*[9]

Similarly, in ruling in favor of the high school football coach, the Court said that the meaning of the Establishment Clause must be interpreted by "'reference to historical practices and understandings.' [T]he line that courts and governments must draw between the permissible and the impermissible" has to "accor[d] with history and faithfully reflec[t] the understanding of the Founding Fathers."

The Court, in these and other cases, embraced originalism in determining the meaning of the Constitution. The liberal justices strongly disagreed with this methodology as well as the results. Not long ago, originalism was regarded as a controversial theory of the far right. The Senate decisively rejected the confirmation of Robert Bork for the Supreme Court in 1987 because his originalist views were regarded as extreme. But now, it is an approach embraced by a majority of the justices.

This also led to a sense that the majority and the dissent were often talking past each other. In a number of cases, the dissent focuses on the practical real-world consequences of the decision—the extent of gun violence in society, the peril of climate change, the impact on women's lives of prohibiting abortions, the risks of opening the door to teacher prayers in public schools. But these are not mentioned in the majority opinions, as the conservative justices are focusing solely on how they believe the Constitution and statutes should be interpreted.

## The Retirement of Stephen Breyer and the Confirmation of Ketanji Brown Jackson

One more significant development of the last year must be noted: the retirement of Justice Stephen Breyer and the confirmation of Justice Ketanji Brown Jackson. For 28 years on the Supreme Court, Justice Stephen Breyer was a moderate liberal on an increasingly conservative Court. He advocated interpreting statutes to achieve their purpose on a Court that moved sharply away from that approach in favor of focusing on the plain language of laws. He stressed looking at pragmatic, real-world consequences on a bench that has become ever more ideological in its rulings. A former professor who specialized in administrative law, he has expressed the need for deference to agencies' expertise at a time when more of the justices are openly hostile to the administrative state.

In some of the most ideologically divided areas of law—abortion, affirmative action, death penalty, gun regulation—Breyer has been consistently and forcefully liberal. This was true in every major case in October Term 2021. But in other areas, most notably the Fourth Amendment and the religion clauses of the First Amendment, sometimes Breyer was with the conservatives, even as the decisive vote. And from a personal perspective, as a lawyer, Breyer was a joy to appear before.

If I had to pick a single Breyer opinion to praise, it would be his dissent, in 2007, in *Parents Involved in Community Schools for Seattle School District No. 1.*[10] The Court, in a 5–4 decision with Chief Justice Roberts authoring the majority opinion, held that public school systems could not use race as a factor in assigning students to schools to achieve diversity.

Breyer wrote a lengthy dissent joined by Justices Stevens, Souter, and Ginsburg. He described how American public schools are increasingly racially segregated and lamented that the Court's decision would place many effective desegregation plans in jeopardy. Breyer declared:

> *The last half century has witnessed great strides toward racial equality, but we have not yet realized the promise of* Brown. *To invalidate the plans under review is to threaten the promise of* Brown. *The plurality's position, I fear, would break that promise. This is a decision that the Court and the Nation will come to regret.*[11]

As I think of Breyer's dissents, I also think of his forceful dissent in 2015 in *Glossip v. Gross,* where he argued that the death penalty is likely unconstitutional.[12] The Court, 5–4, upheld lethal injections in carrying out capital punishment, but Breyer contended that the risks of executing innocent people and the great arbitrariness in the imposition of the death penalty warrant the Court declaring it unconstitutional.

Another notable area of Breyer's dissents was in Second Amendment cases, *District of Columbia v. Heller*, in 2008,[13] and this year, in *New York Rifle and Pistol Association v. Bruen.*[14] His pragmatic approach to the law, focusing on the real-world consequences of judicial decisions, was very much evident in these dissents. From 1791 until that decision, the Supreme Court never had struck down any law as violating the Second Amendment. In the handful of cases dealing with the Second Amendment, the Court said that it was a right to have guns for militia service. In *Heller*, though, the Court ruled, 5–4, that the Second Amendment protects the right of individuals to have guns in their homes for the sake of security and struck down a District of Columbia law prohibiting ownership or possession of handguns.

Justice Scalia's opinion for the Court and Justice Stevens' dissent both focused on the original meaning of the Second Amendment, coming to completely different conclusions. Justice Breyer, though, wrote a dissent focusing on the "facts a court must consider [in] looking at the matter today" in terms of firearm deaths and injuries.[15] In his recent dissent in *New York Rifle and Pistol Association v. Bruen*, Justice Breyer began by describing in detail the human consequences, and deaths, from guns. While the other justices were debating the original meaning of the Second Amendment, Justice Breyer focused on how many people die from guns and how much gun regulations can decrease the fatalities and make a real difference for American society.

One final example of Breyer's liberalism is his consistent votes in favor of protecting reproductive freedom for women. Indeed, he wrote the majority opinion in some of the most recent Supreme Court decisions striking down state laws imposing restrictions on abortion: *Stenberg v. Carhart* (2000),[16] *Whole Woman's Health v. Hellerstedt* (2016),[17] and *June Medical Services LLC v. Russo* (2020).[18] And, of course, he was part of the joint dissent with Justices Sotomayor and Kagan this term in *Dobbs v. Jackson Women's Health Organization.*

But there were notable areas where Breyer joined the conservatives rather than the other liberal justices. One of those places was the Fourth Amendment. In a number of cases, Breyer was the decisive vote in favor of the police. For example, in *Maryland v. King* (2013), Breyer was in the majority in a 5–4 decision—over the dissents of Justices Scalia, Ginsburg, Sotomayor, and Kagan—holding that police may take DNA from a suspect to see if it matches DNA from unsolved crimes in the police database.[19] In *Navarette v. California* (2014), again, Breyer was in the majority in a 5–4 decision over the dissents of the same four justices, holding that police may stop a car solely based on an anonymous tip of erratic driving.[20] And in *Utah v. Strieff* (2016), Breyer joined the four most conservative justices in a 5–3 ruling (this was the year Justice Scalia died) that evidence is admissible despite an illegal stop if police discover that there is an outstanding warrant for the person's arrest.[21]

Another area where Breyer sometimes joined the conservatives was cases involving religion. For example, in *Van Orden v. Perry* (2005)—a case that I argued and lost—Breyer concurred in the judgment and joined with Chief Justice Rehnquist and Justices Scalia, Kennedy, and Thomas, in holding that the Establishment Clause was not violated by a large Ten Commandments monument that sits directly between the Texas State Capitol and the Texas Supreme Court.[22] Breyer was the decisive fifth vote in a 5–4 decision and his focus was pragmatic, evidencing concern about how socially divisive it would be to remove such monuments from public places.

More recently, in *American Legion v. American Humanist Association* (2019), Breyer voted with the majority in holding that a 45-foot cross at a busy intersection on public property did not violate the Establishment Clause.[23] In *Trinity Lutheran v. Comer* (2017), Breyer also was in the majority, holding that Missouri infringed free exercise of religion in denying aid to religious schools for the surfacing of playgrounds when that same assistance was provided to public schools and secular private schools. In both of these cases, liberal Justices Ginsburg and Sotomayor dissented. Breyer, though, joined the liberals in dissent in the two cases since *Trinity Lutheran*—*Espinoza v. Montana Department of Revenue* and *Carson v. Makin*—where the Court went much further and held that the government is constitutionally required to provide religious schools with the same aid it gives to private secular schools.

Many years ago, I was speaking at the Tenth Circuit Judicial Conference and provided a review of the Supreme Court's decisions. I was stunned to see Justice Breyer sitting in a front row. I often have spoken at judicial conferences but rarely have seen a justice attend the law professor's description of the term. At one point, I had planned to sharply criticize the Court's inconsistent rulings in a particular area of law and the lack of needed guidance for lower courts. Even with Breyer there, I decided to go ahead with my remarks as planned. Breyer, on hearing my criticism, demonstrably shrugged in a way that was visible to the audience.

A few years later, the Court's term ended on Thursday, and my Supreme Court review for the Tenth Circuit Judicial Conference was on Friday morning. Breyer brought me copies of the slip opinions from the Thursday decisions. It is the only time in my life I have had Supreme Court decisions hand delivered to me by a justice.

On a number of other occasions, I spoke at judicial conferences, and if Breyer was present, he always attended. After my talk, we always chatted, often about a place where I voiced disagreement with the Court and one of his opinions. I vividly remember these conversations and the cases we talked about. Most of all, I so admired his intellectual engagement and eagerness to discuss the hard issues.

I argued many cases to the Court with Justice Breyer on the bench. Like all advocates, I sometimes found his questions long and occasionally convoluted. But I always so appreciated that his questions expressed exactly what he was concerned about regarding my argument. I was grateful that he gave me the chance to address those concerns, and inevitably his opinions reflected precisely what he raised in oral argument.

Justice Breyer, on the bench and in person, was always courteous to everyone. His opinions never resorted to the sarcasm and invective that some other justices have come to use. In this way, and so many others, he is a model for all who sit on a judicial bench.

Justice Ketanji Brown Jackson was nominated and confirmed to replace Breyer. In the world of law, credentials don't get better than hers. A graduate of Harvard College and Harvard Law School, she clerked for judges in the federal district court and the federal court of appeals, as well as Justice Stephen Breyer in the U.S. Supreme Court. She has extensive practice experience in a variety of settings and has been a federal judge since 2013 in the federal district court and the U.S. Court of Appeals. Lawyers who have appeared before her, liberal and conservative, are effusive in their praise of her as a judge.

Jackson does not change the Court's overall ideological balance; it remains six conservative justices, appointed by Republican presidents, and three liberal justices, appointed by Democratic presidents. But Jackson is 51 years old and should be on the Court for decades. Even though she will not change the ideological balance now, she might do so 10 or 20 years from now. And perhaps, in some cases, her perspective—as the first Black woman and the first justice to have ever worked as a public defender—might sway her colleagues.

## Conclusion

American society is deeply politically polarized. What will it mean that the Supreme Court has come down so decisively on one side of this divide? A Gallup poll in the fall of 2021 showed that the Supreme Court had its lowest approval ratings in history. Only 40 percent expressed approval of the Court, and 53 percent disapproved.[24] A more recent Gallup poll revealed that only 25 percent of the American people expressed confidence in the Supreme Court.[25] This was before the Court overruled *Roe v. Wade*.

It is difficult at any moment to comprehend the long-term significance of events. But no one—conservative or liberal—would deny that this was truly a momentous year in the U.S. Supreme Court. It will shape what happens in the political process, what is litigated and what isn't, and the Court's reputation for many years to come.

## Endnotes

1. Adam Liptak, Court's Term Was Its Most Conservative Since 1931, N.Y. Times, July 2, 2022, at A1.
2. 142 S. Ct. 2228 (2022).
3. 142 S. Ct. 1987 (2022).
4. 142 S. Ct. 2407 (2022).
5. 142 S. Ct. 2587 (2022).
6. *Id.* at 2609.
7. 142 S. Ct. 2111 (2022).
8. *Id.* at 2122.
9. *Id.* at 2126.
10. 551 U.S. 701 (2007).
11. *Id.* at 868 (Breyer, J., dissenting).
12. 576 U.S. 863 (2015).
13. 554 U.S. 570 (2008) (Breyer, J., dissenting).
14. 142 S. Ct. 2111 (2022) (Breyer, J., dissenting).
15. 554 U.S. at 696 (2008) (Breyer, J., dissenting).
16. 530 U.S. 914 (2000).
17. 579 U.S. 582 (2016).
18. 140 S. Ct. 2103 (2020).
19. 569 U.S. 435 (2013).
20. 572 U.S. 393 (2014).
21. 79 U.S. 232 (2016).
22. 545 U.S. 677 (2005).
23. 139 S. Ct. 2067 (2019).
24. Jeffrey M. Jones, Approval of U.S. Supreme Court Down to 40%, a New Low, GALLUP (Sept. 23, 2021), https://news.gallup.com/poll/354908/approval-supreme-court-down-new-low.aspx.
25. Jeffrey M. Jones, Confidence in U.S. Supreme Court Sinks to Historic Low, GALLUP (June 23, 2022), https://news.gallup.com/poll/394103/confidence-supreme-court-sinks-historic-low.aspx.

# 2

# Abortion

October Term 2021 will be most remembered for overruling *Roe v. Wade*.[1] In January 1973, the Court held that the liberty of the due process clause includes the right to privacy and that state laws prohibiting abortion are unconstitutional. The Court ruled that states cannot prohibit abortions prior to viability, the time at which the fetus can survive outside the womb. *Roe* was a 7–2 decision, with the majority opinion written by Justice Harry Blackmun, who had been appointed to the Court by President Richard Nixon. The majority opinion was joined by Nixon appointees Chief Justice Warren Burger and Justice Lewis Powell.

In 1992, in *Planned Parenthood v. Casey*, the Supreme Court reaffirmed *Roe v. Wade* and again held that states cannot prohibit abortions before viability.[2] It was a 5–4 decision, with the five in the majority all justices who had been appointed by Republican presidents: Justice Blackmun, Justice John Paul Stevens (who had been appointed by President Gerald Ford), Justices Sandra Day O'Connor and Anthony Kennedy (who had been appointed by President Ronald Reagan), and Justice David Souter (who had been appointed by President George H.W. Bush).

Over the years since *Roe* and *Casey*, the Supreme Court decided dozens of cases about what types of government regulation of abortion are allowed. For example, the Court upheld waiting periods for abortions and a ban on partial-birth abortions, while it has also ruled that the government was never constitutionally required to fund abortions. But it also struck down requirements for spousal consent or notification for a married woman's abortion and regulations that would have required doctors performing abortions to have admitting privileges at a hospital within 30 miles. A large body of law developed over the last half century as to when and how the government could regulate abortions.

But in *Dobbs v. Jackson Women's Health Organization*, the Supreme Court explicitly overruled *Roe v. Wade* and held that the issue of abortion is left to the political process.[3] Justice Samuel Alito wrote the opinion for the Court, joined by Justices Clarence Thomas, Neil Gorsuch, Brett Kavanaugh, and Amy Coney Barrett. Chief Justice John Roberts concurred in the judgment. He would have upheld the Mississippi law prohibiting abortions after the fifteenth week of pregnancy, but not have reached the question of whether to overrule *Roe*. Justices Stephen Breyer, Sonia Sotomayor, and Elena Kagan wrote a vehement joint dissent.

Although the decision came down on Friday, June 24, something unprecedented occurred about six weeks earlier. On May 2, Politico published a draft of Justice Alito's majority opinion. Secrecy is exalted at the Court. Occasionally there has been a rumor of a decision and sometimes after a ruling is announced there are revelations about the internal deliberations that led to it. But I cannot think of another instance in which a full draft opinion was leaked. The final version was essentially identical to the draft which had been published. In one sense, it made the decision unsurprising. But for the Court to actually overrule the 49-year-old precedent was stunning. What did the Court say and what will it mean?

## The Majority Opinion

*Dobbs* involved a Mississippi law that prohibits abortions after the fifteenth week of pregnancy. Under *Roe* and *Casey*, this is unconstitutional because viability is thought to be the twenty-third or twenty-fourth week of pregnancy. As initially litigated and presented to the Court, the issue was whether states could prohibit abortions at this earlier time in pregnancy. But Mississippi and many *amici* urged the Court to use this case as the vehicle for overruling *Roe*, and the Court did. The Court declared: "We hold that *Roe* and *Casey* must be overruled. The Constitution makes no reference to abortion, and no such right is implicitly protected by any constitutional provision, including the one on which the defenders of *Roe* and *Casey* now chiefly rely—the Due Process Clause of the Fourteenth Amendment."[4]

Justice Alito, writing for the majority, said that a constitutional right exists only if it is in the text of the Constitution or was part of its original meaning or if it has been safeguarded by a long unbroken tradition. The Court said that abortion meets none of these requirements: it obviously is not mentioned in the text and was not part of the original understanding of any constitutional provision. The Court reviewed history, starting with English law before the Constitution, and said, "The inescapable conclusion is that a right to abortion is not deeply rooted in the Nation's history and traditions. On the contrary, an unbroken tradition of prohibiting abortion on pain of criminal punishment persisted from the earliest days of the common law until 1973."[5]

The Court addressed *stare decisis* and said that it did not justify continuing to follow *Roe v. Wade*. The Court said that *Roe* was "egregiously wrong and deeply damaging."[6] It said that "*Roe* was incorrectly decided, but that decision was more than just wrong. It stood on exceptionally weak grounds."[7]

The Court's central conclusion was that the issue of abortion should be left to the political process. The Court declared: "We therefore hold that the Constitution does not confer a right to abortion. *Roe* and *Casey* must be overruled, and the authority to regulate abortion must be returned to the people and their elected representatives."[8]

The Court said that its decision does not place other unenumerated constitutional rights in danger because they, unlike abortion, do not involve "potential life." Justice Alito wrote:

> *But we have stated unequivocally that "[n]othing in this opinion should be understood to cast doubt on precedents that do not concern abortion." We have also explained why that is so: rights regarding contraception and same-sex relationships are inherently different from the right to abortion because the latter (as we have stressed) uniquely involves what* Roe *and* Casey *termed "potential life." Therefore, a right to abortion cannot be justified by a purported analogy to the rights recognized in*

> *those other cases or by "appeals to a broader right to autonomy." It is hard to see how we could be clearer.*[9]

Quite importantly, the Court gave guidance to lower courts as to the standard to use in evaluating regulations of abortion: rational-basis review. Under the rational-basis test, a government action is upheld if it is rationally related to a legitimate government purpose. It is a standard that is deferential to the government; very few laws ever have been struck down by the Court under rational-basis review. The Court stressed exactly this deference:

> *Under our precedents, rational-basis review is the appropriate standard for such challenges. . . . It follows that the States may regulate abortion for legitimate reasons, and when such regulations are challenged under the Constitution, courts cannot "substitute their social and economic beliefs for the judgment of legislative bodies." . . . A law regulating abortion, like other health and welfare laws, is entitled to a "strong presumption of validity."*[10]

The Court was expansive in terms of the interests that will be allowed to justify regulation:

> *It must be sustained if there is a rational basis on which the legislature could have thought that it would serve legitimate state interests. These legitimate interests include respect for and preservation of prenatal life at all stages of development; the protection of maternal health and safety; the elimination of particularly gruesome or barbaric medical procedures; the preservation of the integrity of the medical profession; the mitigation of fetal pain; and the prevention of discrimination on the basis of race, sex, or disability.*[11]

Justices Thomas and Kavanaugh each wrote concurring opinions. Justice Thomas disagreed with the Court's reassurance that other constitutional rights are not in jeopardy. He said that there is no such thing as substantive due process and no rights should be protected under it. He was explicit in calling for the overruling of landmark precedents safeguarding the right to purchase and use contraceptives, the right to engage in private consensual same-sex sexual activity, and the right to same-sex marriage. He wrote: "For that reason, in future cases, we should reconsider all of this Court's substantive due process precedents, including Griswold, Lawrence, and Obergefell. Because any substantive due process decision is 'demonstrably erroneous,' we have a duty to 'correct the error' established in those precedents."[12] He called for "overruling these demonstrably erroneous decisions."[13]

Justice Kavanaugh wrote separately to stress that the contentious issue of abortion should be left to the political process. He said: "On the question of abortion, the Constitution is therefore neither pro-life nor pro-choice. The Constitution is neutral and leaves the issue for the people and their elected representatives to resolve through the democratic process in the States or Congress—like the numerous other difficult questions of American social and economic policy that the Constitution does not address."[14]

He also wanted to offer reassurance, quite the opposite of Justice Thomas, that overruling *Roe* would not put other constitutional rights in jeopardy. He specifically spoke of the cases that Justice Thomas mentioned such as *Griswold v. Connecticut* (1965); *Eisenstadt v. Baird* (1972); *Loving v. Virginia* (1967); and *Obergefell v. Hodges* (2015). He wrote: "I emphasize what the Court today states: Overruling *Roe* does *not* mean the overruling of those precedents, and does *not* threaten or cast doubt on those precedents."[15]

He also addressed an issue sure to arise in the future: may a state prohibit a woman from leaving the state to get an abortion? A bill was introduced into the Missouri legislature to do just this. But Justice Kavanaugh wrote: "may a State bar a resident of that State from traveling to another State to obtain an abortion? In my view, the answer is no based on the constitutional right to interstate travel."[16]

Chief Justice Roberts concurred in the judgment and said that he would uphold the Mississippi law and allow states to ban abortions after the fifteenth week of pregnancy, but not reach the question of whether to overrule *Roe*.[17] He sharply criticized drawing the line at viability as to when states can prohibit abortions and would overrule that aspect of *Roe* and

*Casey*. He said that the viability was an arbitrary line and not one followed in other countries. But he said that there was no reason to go further than that: "But that is all I would say, out of adherence to a simple yet fundamental principle of judicial restraint: If it is not necessary to decide more to dispose of a case, then it is necessary *not* to decide more."[18]

Justices Breyer, Sotomayor, and Kagan wrote an unusual joint dissenting opinion and it was, as was expected, passionate and angry. They stressed that some states already had banned abortion from the moment of conception and that these laws would now go into effect. They focused on what this will mean for women's lives and stated:

> *Some States have enacted laws extending to all forms of abortion procedure, including taking medication in one's own home. They have passed laws without any exceptions for when the woman is the victim of rape or incest. Under those laws, a woman will have to bear her rapist's child or a young girl her father's—no matter if doing so will destroy her life. So too, after today's ruling, some States may compel women to carry to term a fetus with severe physical anomalies—for example, one afflicted with Tay-Sachs disease, sure to die within a few years of birth. States may even argue that a prohibition on abortion need make no provision for protecting a woman from risk of death or physical harm. Across a vast array of circumstances, a State will be able to impose its moral choice on a woman and coerce her to give birth to a child.*[19]

They explained that the effect will be that women in states where abortion is illegal will travel to places where abortion is allowed if they have the resources to do so, but that poor women and teenagers again will face the cruel choice between an unwanted child and an unsafe back-alley abortion. Because of the correlation of race and poverty in the United States, it is especially women of color who will be in this situation.

They said that *Roe* is part of a larger fabric of constitutional cases protecting aspects of privacy and autonomy, and that overruling it places these other rights in jeopardy. They explained that cases protecting a right to contraception, *Griswold v. Connecticut* (1965)[20] and *Eisenstadt v. Baird* (1972),[21] and those safeguarding rights of same-sex intimacy and marriage, *Lawrence v. Texas* (2003)[22] and *Obergefell v. Hodges* (2015)[23] respectively, "are all part of the same constitutional fabric, protecting autonomous decisionmaking over the most personal of life decisions."[24] They explained that under the criteria set forth by the majority, none of these rights are deserving of constitutional protection because none are in the text or were part of the original understanding or were part of a long unbroken tradition. They obviously were not convinced by the Court's and Justice Kavanaugh's reassurance that these rights are different because they do not involve "potential life."

The dissent defended *Roe* and its recognition that laws prohibiting abortion infringe a woman's liberty. They argued that viability was a desirable compromise between competing positions and that the Mississippi law should have been declared unconstitutional.

The dissenting justices stressed *stare decisis* and lamented the Court's abandoning precedent. They wrote:

> *The majority has no good reason for the upheaval in law and society it sets off.* Roe *and* Casey *have been the law of the land for decades, shaping women's expectations of their choices when an unplanned pregnancy occurs. Women have relied on the availability of abortion both in structuring their relationships and in planning their lives. The legal framework* Roe *and* Casey *developed to balance the competing interests in this sphere has proved workable in courts across the country. No recent developments, in either law or fact, have eroded or cast doubt on those precedents. Nothing, in short, has changed.*[25]

The dissent saw overruling *Roe* as greatly damaging the Court's public esteem. At the oral argument, Justice Sotomayor asked how the Court could survive the "stench" of what would be perceived by the public as a purely political decision.[26]

The dissented powerfully concluded: "In overruling *Roe* and *Casey*, this Court betrays its guiding principles. With sorrow—for this Court, but more, for the many millions of American women who have today lost a fundamental constitutional protection—we dissent."[27]

## Implications

*Dobbs* means that the issue of abortion is left to the political process, for the states and perhaps Congress. The Court explicitly says that overruling *Roe* means that no longer will courts enforce a limit on what states and Congress can do in regulating abortion. States will be able to prohibit abortion or allow abortion, whatever they choose. Over half of the states are likely to outlaw all or virtually all abortions. Some of these laws will prohibit abortions from the moment of conception. Many will have no exceptions for instances where the pregnancy resulted from rape or incest.

But abortion will remain legal in many states, such as California, New York, Illinois, and Connecticut. As the dissent explained, women who want to terminate their pregnancies and live in states where abortion will be illegal will travel, if they have the resources to do so, to states where abortion is allowed. It is poor women and often teenagers who will have to choose between an unwanted child and an unsafe abortion. Funds are being created in states like California to pay for women who cannot afford to travel to receive an abortion. But I also expect that some states that prohibit abortion will try to adopt laws forbidding women from leaving the state to obtain an abortion. A bill already has been introduced into the Missouri legislature to do this and I expect that other states will adopt such laws. The constitutionality of such efforts is uncertain, although Justice Kavanaugh in his concurring opinion expressed his doubts about such statutes.

States, though, can regulate only if Congress does not enact a law for the entire country. Congress, for example, could adopt a law creating a right to abortion for all women in the United States. Congress could use its power to regulate commerce among the states, concluding that abortions are economic activity because they are a service that is paid for and that cumulatively across the country allowing abortions has a substantial effect on interstate commerce. Or when there is a Republican president and a Republican Congress, a law might be adopted to prohibit all abortions. About 20 years ago, Congress adopted the federal Partial-Birth Abortion Act that outlaws a particular abortion procedure. If Congress were to prohibit all abortions, California and other states would be powerless and no longer could allow the procedure. Practically speaking, such a bill protecting the right to abortion or prohibiting all abortions is likely to pass the House of Representatives, but not the Senate because of the filibuster. But if either party were willing to change the rules of the filibuster to allow passage of the bill by a majority vote, such a federal law is likely when Congress and the president are controlled by the same political party.

At first glance the Court's decision in *Dobbs* restores the law to what it was before 1973 when *Roe v. Wade* was decided. But there are also ways that the situation is much different from 50 years ago. Abortion has become a political issue in a way that it was not before *Roe v. Wade*. Conservative politicians who have been railing against abortion rights for decades are not going to give up this political issue. There likely will be far more aggressive enforcement of prohibitions of abortions than occurred prior to 1973. Expect to see doctors and women prosecuted for violating state laws prohibiting abortion much more frequently than occurred prior to *Roe*. The prospect of such aggressive enforcement may make doctors more reluctant to perform abortions, even when the life of the women is in jeopardy.

Some states likely will adopt laws to eliminate forms of birth control that take effect after conception, such as IUDs and the morning after pill. There will be regulation of medical procedures, such as in vitro fertilization, with some states perhaps adopting laws requiring all embryos to be implanted. All of this will lead to litigation and the Court will have to decide if there are any constitutional limits on the states or if the matter is truly entirely left to the political process.

At the same time, medically induced abortions now are possible and account for over half of all abortions. This will make it harder for states to prohibit abortions as pills can be sent across state lines. States that outlaw abortions will make consuming these pills a crime, though enforcement will be difficult. Also, there will be much more organized efforts to raise money to help women in states where abortion is illegal to have access to the procedure.

There is also the issue of whether there must be an exception for abortion where the life of the woman is in danger and what this will require. Some states do not have an exception for pregnancies resulting from rape or incest, and the constitutionality of those laws will be challenged.

Justice Alito's opinion for the Court says that *Roe* was "egregiously wrong" because it protects a right that was not included in the text of the Constitution, protected by the original meaning of the Constitution, or traditionally safeguarded as a constitutional right.

But by that reasoning, countless other Supreme Court decisions protecting basic aspects of privacy and autonomy were wrongly decided as well. For example, it was not until 1965, in *Griswold v. Connecticut*, that the Court held that the Constitution protects a right to purchase and use contraceptives. It, too, is not a right in the text of the Constitution; it was not contemplated when the document was ratified, nor was it historically protected.

Or consider the right to marry. It wasn't until 1967, in *Loving v. Virginia*,[28] and 2015, in *Obergefell v. Hodges*,[29] that the Court protected a constitutional right to marry, striking down laws prohibiting interracial marriage in the former case and laws forbidding same-sex marriage in the latter. But this right cannot be found in the text, the original meaning, or tradition.

Likewise, the Court has protected the right to procreate, the right to custody of one's children, the right to keep the family together, the right of parents to control the upbringing of their children, the right of competent adults to refuse medical care, and the right of consenting adults to engage in same-sex sexual activity under the liberty of the due process clause. These rights, too, cannot be justified under the Court's approach.

Justice Alito's opinion for the Court and Justice Kavanaugh's opinion stressed that these other precedents are not in danger because they do not involve "potential life." But is this reassurance persuasive? Justice Alito vehemently dissented in *Obergefell* and it surely would not have been decided the same way by the current Court. Why believe that the conservative justices will give more weight to *stare decisis* as to these rights than it did with regard to abortion?

Finally, abortion will come to dominate our political process like never before. State judicial elections—and 39 states have some form of judicial election—will focus on abortion because state judges can protect rights under state constitutions. Elections for state legislatures, city councils, and members of Congress often will focus on abortion rights more than ever before as the issue now has been left to the political process.

## Conclusion

Freedom and equality have expanded enormously over the course of American history, which makes the ending of a constitutional right virtually unprecedented. In *Dobbs v. Jackson Women's Health Organization*, the Court overruled a half century of decisions protecting a constitutional right of women to choose whether to end their pregnancies.

Every woman of reproductive age in the United States has spent her lifetime possessing a constitutional right that no longer exists. Women with unwanted pregnancies will continue to seek abortions. Some will still get them safely. Some will die or be maimed getting them unsafely. Some will have unwanted children. The implications of *Dobbs* are enormous, most of all, for women's lives.

## Endnotes

1. 410 U.S. 113 (1973). There also was another case concerning abortion—*Whole Woman's Health v. Jackson*—that involved Texas's SB 8 that prohibited abortions after the sixth week of pregnancy and authorized civil suits against doctors and those who aid and abet abortions. The Court's holding was about when state officers can be sued if they play no role in enforcing a law. It is discussed in Chapter 7 on Federal Jurisdiction.
2. 505 U.S. 833 (1992).
3. 142 S. Ct. 2228 (2022).
4. *Id.* at 2242.
5. *Id.* at 2253-54.
6. *Id.* at 2265.
7. *Id.* at 2266.
8. *Id.* at 2279.
9. *Id.* at 2280 (internal citations omitted).
10. *Id.* at 2383-84 (internal citations omitted).
11. *Id* at 2284 (internal citations omitted).
12. *Id.* at 2301 (Thomas, J., concurring) (internal citations omitted).
13. *Id.*
14. *Id.* at 2305 (Kavanaugh, J., concurring).
15. *Id.* at 2309.
16. *Id.*
17. *Id.* at 2310 (Roberts, J., concurring in the judgment).

18. *Id* at 2311.
19. *Id.* at 2318 (Breyer, Sotomayor, and Kagan dissenting).
20. 381 U.S. 479.
21. 405 U.S. 438.
22. 539 U.S. 558.
23. 576 U.S. 644.
24. 142 S. Ct. at 2319.
25. *Id.*
26. Transcript of Oral Argument at 15, Dobbs v. Jackson Women's Health Organization,142 S. Ct. 2228 (2022) (No. 19-1392).
27. 142 S. Ct. at 2350.
28. 388 U.S. 1 (1967).
29. 576 U.S. 644 (2015).

3

# Administrative Law

It has been widely predicted that the conservative Supreme Court will change administrative law and limit the power of administrative agencies. In October Term 2021, the Court provided one direction this might take: a relatively new legal principle called "the major questions doctrine." This is the principle that Congress must give agencies clear direction when acting on questions of major economic or social significance. Absent such guidance on a major question, the agency's action is invalid.

In *West Virginia v. Environmental Protection Agency*, the Court expressly relied on the major questions doctrine to limit the authority of the Environmental Protection Agency to regulate greenhouse gas emissions from power plants.[1] In *National Federation of Independent Businesses v. Department of Labor, Occupational Safety and Health Administration*, the Court invalidated an emergency temporary standard promulgated by the Biden administration that required those working in places with more than 100 employees to be vaccinated against COVID-19 or tested on a weekly basis.[2] Although the majority opinion did not expressly mention it, Justice Neil Gorsuch, in a concurring opinion, invoked the major question doctrine saying that it explained the Court's holding. By contrast, in *Biden v. Missouri*, the Court upheld a federal requirement that facilities receiving federal Medicare or Medicaid funds require that their workers be tested.

The two cases striking down agency action on the grounds that there was not sufficient direction from Congress are important. They each invalidated administrative actions in areas of great social significance, climate change and vaccinations. But even more crucial, they provide a path for challenges to countless agency actions in the lower courts.

## *West Virginia v. Environmental Protection Agency*

*West Virginia v. Environmental Protection Agency* involves the authority of the EPA to regulate power plants to limit their greenhouse gas emissions. Coal-fired power plants are a major source of the pollution that significantly contributes to climate change.

The Obama administration adopted an aggressive approach, known as the Clean Power Plan, to limit these pollutants from coal-fired power plants across the country. The goal was to decrease the amount of energy produced by coal-fired power plants in the United States. The Trump administration rescinded the Clean Power Plan and adopted its own Affordable Clean Energy Plan, which was far more permissive in allowing pollution.

The U.S. Court of Appeals for the District of Columbia Circuit ruled that the Trump administration failed to follow proper procedures in rescinding the Obama-era plan and enacting its own approach. West Virginia and several coal companies sought Supreme Court review.

The Supreme Court, in a 6–3 decision, ruled that the EPA is limited in its ability to regulate greenhouse gas emissions from power plants. Chief Justice John Roberts wrote the opinion for the majority, joined by the other conservative justices. Justice Elena Kagan wrote the dissent for the three liberal justices.

The Biden administration urged the Supreme Court not to take the case and then, once taken, urged the Court to dismiss it.[3] The EPA has clarified that it does not intend to revive the Clean Power Plan or implement the Affordable Clean Energy Plan. The Biden administration has announced that it will produce its own, new approach. In other words, the Obama administration's Clean Power Plan is not law, the Trump administration's Affordable Clean Energy (ACE) rule is not law, and the Biden administration has not promulgated any rule on the subject. There are currently no regulations on power plant greenhouse gas emissions. In light of this, the Biden administration argued that the case should not have been decided, asserting that the Court does not have the authority to judicially review future, potential, or hypothetical administrative regulations.

The Supreme Court expressly rejected this argument and drew a distinction between standing and mootness. The Court concluded that the states were injured by the earlier rule and thus had standing to challenge it. The question then, the Court observed, was whether the case should be dismissed on mootness grounds. There is an exception to the mootness doctrine, "voluntary cessation," which provides that cases will not be dismissed as moot if the defendant voluntarily halts that allegedly impermissible behavior but is free to resume it at any time. Chief Justice Roberts, writing for the majority, explained:

> *But "voluntary cessation does not moot a case" unless it is "absolutely clear that the allegedly wrongful behavior could not reasonably be expected to recur." Here the Government "nowhere suggests that if this litigation is resolved in its favor it will not" reimpose emissions limits predicated on generation shifting; indeed, it "vigorously defends" the legality of such an approach. We do not dismiss a case as moot in such circumstances. The case thus remains justiciable, and we may turn to the merits.*[4]

Under the Clean Air Act, the EPA is authorized to determine the "best system of emission reduction" that, taking into account cost, health, and other factors, it finds "has been adequately demonstrated." The EPA then quantifies "the degree of emission limitation achievable" if that best system were applied to the covered source. The central issue in the case is whether restructuring the nation's overall mix of electricity generation—to transition from 38 percent to 27 percent coal by 2030—can be the best system of emission reduction within the meaning of the Clean Air Act.

The Court said that the question of agency authority is usually determined by looking at the statute empowering the administrative action. But the Court explained that "our precedent teaches that there are 'extraordinary cases' that call for a different approach—cases in which the 'history and the breadth of the authority that [the agency] has asserted,' and the 'economic and political significance' of that assertion, provide a 'reason to hesitate before concluding that Congress' meant to confer such authority."[5]

The Court then said that Congress must be specific in empowering the federal agency to act when it comes to such major questions. Chief Justice Roberts wrote:

> *Thus, in certain extraordinary cases, both separation of powers principles and a practical understanding of legislative intent make us "reluctant to read into ambiguous statutory text" the delegation claimed to be lurking there. To convince us otherwise, something more than a merely plausible textual basis for the agency action is necessary. The agency instead must point to "clear congressional authorization" for the power it claims.*[6]

It is notable that the Court grounds the major questions doctrine, in part, on separation of powers considerations. In other words, it is interpreting the Constitution as requiring that Congress provide clear direction on "major questions" and saying that without it, an agency action is invalid in such areas.

The Court disagreed with the dissent's objection to the invention of the major questions doctrine. It said, "As for the major questions doctrine label, it took hold because it refers to an identifiable body of law that has developed over a series of significant cases all addressing a particular and recurring problem: agencies asserting highly consequential power beyond what Congress could reasonably be understood to have granted."[7]

The Court said that "under our precedents, this is a major questions case."[8] The Court said that the EPA was using a long-existing statute to claim "an unheralded power" to "substantially restructure the American energy market" and achieve a "transformative expansion in [its] regulatory authority."[9] The Court found little indication that Congress meant to give the EPA such broad authority. Chief Justice Roberts concluded the majority opinion:

> *Capping carbon dioxide emissions at a level that will force a nationwide transition away from the use of coal to generate*

> *electricity may be a sensible "solution to the crisis of the day." But it is not plausible that Congress gave EPA the authority to adopt on its own such a regulatory scheme in Section 111(d). A decision of such magnitude and consequence rests with Congress itself, or an agency acting pursuant to a clear delegation from that representative body.*[10]

Justice Gorsuch wrote a concurring opinion joined by Justice Alito, arguing that the major questions doctrine was based on constitutional requirements of separation of powers. He began his opinion by stating:

> *To resolve today's case the Court invokes the major questions doctrine. Under that doctrine's terms, administrative agencies must be able to point to "clear congressional authorization" when they claim the power to make decisions of vast "economic and political significance." Like many parallel clear-statement rules in our law, this one operates to protect foundational constitutional guarantees.*[11]

The dissenting justices, not surprisingly, saw the case very differently. It is telling that Justice Kagan began her dissent by describing the enormous peril to the planet from climate change: "Today, the Court strips the Environmental Protection Agency (EPA) of the power Congress gave it to respond to 'the most pressing environmental challenge of our time.'"[12]

Unlike the majority, which says nothing about the dangers of climate change, the dissent focuses on it:

> *Climate change's causes and dangers are no longer subject to serious doubt . . . [t]he Earth is now warmer than at any time "in the history of modern civilization," with the six warmest years on record all occurring in the last decade. The rise in temperatures brings with it "increases in heat-related deaths," "coastal inundation and erosion," "more frequent and intense hurricanes, floods, and other extreme weather events," "drought," "destruction of ecosystems," and "potentially significant disruptions of food production."*[13]

The dissent argued with the Biden administration that there was no need for the Court to address the EPA authority because no rules for power plants were in existence. On the merits, the dissent argued that the Clean Air Act was sufficiently specific in authorizing EPA action. Justice Kagan objected to the "major questions doctrine" as a basis for the decision and said, "[t]he Court has never even used the term 'major questions doctrine' before."[14]

Justice Kagan chastised the majority for ignoring the textual authority for the EPA to act and the Court's requiring more than that. She wrote:

> *Some years ago, I remarked that "[w]e're all textualists now." It seems I was wrong. The current Court is textualist only when being so suits it. When that method would frustrate broader goals, special canons like the "major questions doctrine" magically appear as get-out-of-text-free cards. Today, one of those broader goals makes itself clear: Prevent agencies from doing important work, even though that is what Congress directed. That anti-administrative-state stance shows up in the majority opinion, and it suffuses the concurrence.*[15]

The dissent's concern, in addition to the implications for climate change, is that this will lead to challenges to many other federal statutes. Justice Kagan explained that broad delegations to agencies are often needed, and the major questions doctrine will provide a basis for businesses to challenge countless federal regulations.

## Vaccine Mandates

On January 14, 2022, the Court decided two cases concerning vaccine mandates imposed by the Biden administration. *National Federation of Independent Businesses v. Department of Labor, Occupational Safety and Health Administration* involved a rule that mandates employers with more than 100 workers to require vaccinations or weekly COVID-19 tests of their employees.[16] It was estimated that this would apply to about 84 million workers in the United States. The Occupational Safety and Health

Administration (OSHA) said this emergency rule would have saved over 6,500 lives and prevented over 250,000 hospitalizations in six months.

OSHA created the workplace mandate as an emergency temporary standard, which can be adopted when "employees are exposed to grave danger from exposure to substances or agents determined to be toxic or physically harmful or from new hazards."

On December 17, the U.S. Court of Appeals for the Sixth Circuit, in a 2–1 decision, ruled in favor of the Biden administration and upheld the mandate. The court explained that "Given OSHA's clear and exercised authority to regulate viruses, OSHA necessarily has the authority to regulate infectious diseases that are not unique to the workplace . . . OSHA has demonstrated the pervasive danger that COVID-19 poses to workers—unvaccinated workers in particular—in their workplaces."[17]

But the Supreme Court reversed, in a 6–3 decision, with the six conservative justices comprising the majority. Although the Court did not use the phrase "major questions doctrine," its reasoning was much the same as in its subsequent ruling in *West Virginia v. EPA*. In a per curiam opinion, the Court said, "this is no 'everyday exercise of federal power.' It is instead a significant encroachment into the lives—and health—of a vast number of employees. We expect Congress to speak clearly when authorizing an agency to exercise powers of vast economic and political significance."[18]

The majority stressed that "OSHA is limited to regulating 'work-related dangers'" and explicitly rejected the government's argument that the risk of contracting COVID-19 qualifies as such a danger.[19] The Court concluded, "although COVID-19 is a risk that occurs in many workplaces, it is not an *occupational* hazard in most. COVID-19 can and does spread at home, in schools, during sporting events, and everywhere else that people gather."[20] The majority stressed the unprecedented sweep of the regulation.

Justice Gorsuch wrote a concurring opinion, joined by Justices Thomas and Alito. He said that the Court was applying the major questions doctrine and requiring that Congress give clear instructions to agencies dealing with issues of major social or political significance. As he did several months later in a concurring opinion in *West Virginia v. EPA*, Justice Gorsuch argued that separation of powers requires that the Court enforce the major questions doctrine.

> *Why does the major questions doctrine matter? It ensures that the national government's power to make the laws that govern us remains where Article I of the Constitution says it belongs—with the people's elected representatives. If administrative agencies seek to regulate the daily lives and liberties of millions of Americans, the doctrine says, they must at least be able to trace that power to a clear grant of authority from Congress.*[21]

There was a joint dissenting opinion of Justices Breyer, Sotomayor, and Kagan. They began by describing the devastation and danger of COVID-19, emphasizing how it had killed hundreds of thousands of Americans. They argued that if the sweep of the rule is unprecedented, that is because the dangers from COVID-19 also are unprecedented.

The dissenters found clear statutory authority for OSHA to deal with the risk of spreading COVID-19 in the workplace. The majority ruled that because COVID-19 also occurs outside the workplace, OSHA cannot regulate it, but the dissenters argued that there is nothing in the OSHA statute that creates this limit on OSHA's power. As the dissenting justices observed: "OSHA has long regulated risks that arise both inside and outside of the workplace. For example, OSHA has issued, and applied to nearly all workplaces, rules combating risks of fire, faulty electrical installations, and inadequate emergency exits—even though the dangers prevented by those rules arise not only in workplaces.[22]

The Court's majority said that this regulation is unprecedented. But if the policy is unique, the dissent replied that is because it is in response to an unprecedented crisis: the deadliest pandemic in American history. The dissent wrote:

> *If OSHA's Standard is far-reaching—applying to many millions of American workers—it no more than reflects the scope of the crisis. The Standard responds to a workplace health emergency unprecedented in the agency's history: an infectious disease that has already killed hundreds of thousands and sickened millions; that is most easily transmitted in the shared indoor spaces that are the hallmark of American working life; and that spreads mostly without regard to differences in occupation or industry.*[23]

The dissent stressed that it should be for OSHA and not the courts to decide what needs to be done to limit the spread of COVID-19 in the workplace.

A second decision on January 14, *Biden v. Missouri*, upheld a vaccination requirement for health care workers.[24] The regulation was adopted by the Centers for Medicare and Medicaid Services in the Department of Health and Human Services. It requires all health care workers at facilities that participate in the Medicare and Medicaid programs to be fully vaccinated against COVID-19 unless eligible for a medical or religious exemption. It covers about 10 million workers. Twenty-six states, all led by Republican officials, brought several lawsuits challenging this rule.

The Court, 5–4, upheld this, with Chief Justice Roberts and Justice Kavanaugh joining the liberal justices to create the majority. It is hard to reconcile that these two decisions came from the same Court on the same day. In this decision, the Court, again in a per curiam opinion, recognized the grave danger posed by COVID-19 and noted that although the regulation was unprecedented, the nation has never had to "address an infection problem of this scale and scope before."[25] The Court noted that vaccination requirements for other infectious diseases have long existed, even if not mandated by the federal government. The statutes, in this case, were no more explicit in providing the agency authority to adopt the regulations than in the OSHA case.

Nothing explains the opposite results other than Roberts and Kavanaugh seeing the cases differently. The other seven justices saw no difference. Perhaps Roberts and Kavanaugh saw distinction because this regulation applies to only 10 million workers, rather than the over 80 million employees affected by the OSHA rule. Perhaps it is because this rule is a condition imposed on those receiving federal funds where they see the federal government having more latitude to act.

## Implications

What explains the decisions from this term concerning administrative law, and what are they likely to mean? Perhaps the decisions reflect a vast difference between conservatives and liberals about the underlying issues.

Conservatives see climate change as much less a problem than do liberals. Likewise, the decisions may reflect the politicization of the pandemic. A national poll by the University of South Florida at the time of the decisions about the vaccine mandates[26] found that 50 percent of Democrats, but only 15 percent of Republicans, regarded COVID-19 as the most serious problem facing the country. The poll found that 88 percent of Democrats, but only 22 percent of Republicans, favored the OSHA vaccination requirement. Over 90 percent of Democrats but only 60 percent of Republicans are vaccinated.

But there is also something else underlying the Court's decision: differing views of administrative agencies. The majority in *West Virginia v. EPA* and *National Federation of Independent Business* stressed the need to limit the power of federal agencies. The dissent sees the benefit of empowering them to deal with the urgent crises of climate change and COVID-19.

My guess is that few judges or lawyers had heard of the major questions doctrine until very recently. The Court has never defined what constitutes a "major question" or what is sufficiently specific to meet this standard. Nor are there any criteria for what makes a decision one of "vast economic or political significance." This opens the door to challenges to many federal laws that empower federal agencies to deal with various issues, including those regulating the environment and involving public health and safety. I expect there will be hundreds of cases where those being regulated will argue that the agency action is occurring in an area of social and political importance, but that Congress was not sufficiently specific in its grant of authority to the agency. This will be a major area of litigation for years to come.

## Endnotes

1. 142 S. Ct. 2587 (2022).
2. 142 S. Ct. 661 (2022).
3. I should disclose that I also wrote an amicus brief on behalf of Senator Sheldon Whitehouse (and three other Democratic Senators) urging the Court to dismiss the case on this basis. *See* Brief of U.S. Senators Sheldon Whitehouse et al. as Amici Curiae in Support of Respondents, West Virginia v. Environmental Protection Agency, 142 S. Ct. 2587 (2022) (No. 20-1530), 2021 WL 6693202.
4. 142 S. Ct. at 2607.

5. *Id.* at 2608.
6. *Id.* at 2609.
7. *Id.*
8. *Id.* at 2610.
9. *Id.* (internal citations omitted).
10. *Id.* at 2616.
11. *Id.* (Gorsuch, J., concurring).
12. *Id.* at 2626 (Kagan, J., dissenting).
13. *Id.*
14. *Id.* at 2634.
15. *Id.* at 2641.
16. 142 S. Ct. 661 (2022).
17. In re MCP NO. 165, 21 F.4th 357, 377 (6th Cir. 2021).
18. 142 S. Ct. at 665 (2022).
19. *Id.*
20. *Id.*
21. *Id.* at 668 (Gorsuch, J., dissenting).
22. *Id.* at 673 (Breyer, J.; Kagan, J.; Sotomayor, J., dissenting).
23. *Id.* at 675.
24. 142 S. Ct. 647 (2022).
25. *Id.* at 653.
26. Scott Powers, *Poll finds huge Democratic, Republican divides on pandemic, corruption, race, debt*, Florida Politics (Jan. 14, 2022), https://floridapolitics.com/archives/486279-poll-finds-huge-democratic-republican-divides-on-pandemic-corruption-race-debt/.

# 4

# Civil Rights

There were several civil rights cases decided in October 2021. They involved important issues in civil rights litigation, including the scope of qualified immunity, the ability to sue federal officers for money damages for constitutional violations, whether there can be civil suits when police fail to provide *Miranda* warnings, and the requirements for constitutional claims for malicious prosecution. In all but the last, the Supreme Court followed the pattern from recent years and ruled against civil rights plaintiffs, narrowing the ability to sue for constitutional violations.

## Qualified Immunity

Two unanimous Supreme Court decisions from early in the term show that the justices are continuing to broadly interpret qualified immunity and limit suits against government officials, especially police officers. Perhaps this will help fuel pressure on Congress to enact a law to revise qualified immunity, but so far, such efforts have passed the House of Representatives and stalled in the Senate.

All government officers sued for money damages can raise an immunity defense. Although 42 U.S.C. §1983 is written in the language of strict liability, authorizing recovery against any person acting under color of law who violates the Constitution or federal laws, the Supreme Court has created immunity as a defense. Some government officials—such as judges for their judicial acts, prosecutors for their prosecutorial acts, and legislators for their legislative acts—have absolute immunity to suits for money damages. All government officials who do not have absolute immunity have qualified immunity.

The Supreme Court has said that officers performing discretionary functions are protected by qualified immunity unless they violate clearly established law that every reasonable officer should know.[1] In *District of Columbia v. Wesby*, in 2018, the Court explained: "In other words, existing law must have placed the constitutionality of the officer's conduct 'beyond debate.' This demanding standard protects 'all but the plainly incompetent or those who knowingly violate the law.'"[2] The Court stressed that well established law must specify that the conduct of the officer is unlawful: "The 'clearly established' standard also requires that the legal principle clearly prohibit the officer's conduct in the particular circumstances before him. The rule's contours must be so well defined that it is 'clear to a reasonable officer that his conduct was unlawful in the situation he confronted.'"[3]

Many on both the right and the left of the political spectrum have sharply criticized the Supreme Court's qualified immunity jurisprudence as making it enormously difficult for victims of constitutional violations to recover for their injuries. Fifth Circuit Judge Don Willett, a Trump appointee to the federal court of appeals, wrote of his "disquiet over the kudzu-like creep of the modern immunity regime."[4] He said:

> *Section 1983 meets Catch-22. Plaintiffs must produce precedent even as fewer courts are producing precedent. Important constitutional questions go unanswered precisely because those questions are yet unanswered. Courts then rely on that judicial silence to conclude there's no equivalent case on the books. No precedent = no clearly established law = no liability. An Escherian Stairwell. Heads defendants win, tails plaintiffs lose.*[5]

In November 2020, in *Taylor v. Riojas*, the Supreme Court rejected qualified immunity, leading to speculation that the Court was responding to its critics by lessening the bar to recovery by plaintiffs.[6] The case involved a prisoner who had been placed in horrific conditions, but the lower courts found that the prison officials were protected by qualified immunity because of the absence of a case on point with virtually identical facts. The Court, in a 7–1 decision, reversed and stressed that there does not need to be a case on point: officers can be held liable so long as they have "fair warning" that their conduct is unconstitutional.

However, the two recent decisions by the Court—*Rivas-Villegas v. Cortesluna* and *City of Talequah v. Bond*—indicate that the speculation about an overall shift in approach to qualified immunity was unfounded. Both cases involved claims against police officers for excessive force. In each, the Court reversed a federal court of appeals and found qualified immunity, stressing the absence of a case with sufficiently similar facts.

In *Rivas-Villegas v. Cortesluna*, police responded to a domestic violence call.[7] Ramon Cortesluna, the suspect, came out of the house and was shot twice by the police when he put his hands down after being told not to do so. Officer Daniel Rivas-Villegas then pushed him onto the ground and pressed his knee against Cortesluna's back so that a colleague could handcuff him.

Cortesluna sued the officers for excessive force. The federal district court concluded that the force used by both officers was reasonable and that the officers were entitled to qualified immunity. The Ninth Circuit found that the firing of the shots with beanbag rounds was protected by qualified immunity, but that it was excessive force for a police officer to press his knee into the back of a suspect lying face down on the ground hard enough to cause an injury.

The Supreme Court unanimously reversed in a per curiam opinion and concluded that the officer was protected from liability by qualified immunity. The Court stressed the absence of a case with sufficiently similar facts. The Court declared: "Even assuming that controlling Circuit precedent clearly establishes law for purposes of §1983, [prior precedent] did not give fair notice to Rivas-Villegas. He is thus entitled to qualified immunity."[8] The Court said, "[a]lthough "his Court's case law does not require a case directly on point for a right to be clearly established, existing precedent must have placed the statutory or constitutional question beyond debate."[9]

It is significant that the justices once more noted that they had not yet decided whether anything other than a Supreme Court decision can create clearly established law. This suggests the possibility of a future decision holding that only Supreme Court precedents can create a basis for liability. Although the Court says that there does not need to be a case "directly on point," it then finds qualified immunity entirely because no prior decision had sufficiently similar facts.

The Court's other decision, *City of Talequah v. Bond*, similarly arose from a domestic violence situation.[10] Police were called by a woman to remove her ex-husband, Dominic Rollice, from her home. The police confronted Rollice in a garage. While talking to the police, Rollice picked up a hammer. When Rollice disobeyed the police order to drop the hammer, police shot and killed him.

Rollice's estate sued the police for excessive force. The federal district court ruled in favor of the officers, but the U.S. Court of Appeals for the Tenth Circuit reversed. The Court of Appeals found that the police used excessive force and were not protected by qualified immunity. The Court of Appeals found that the officers were not in danger from the hammer and the use of deadly force was unreasonable under the circumstances.

The Supreme Court again reversed in a per curiam opinion. Once more, the Court stressed the absence of a case with sufficiently similar facts. It stated: "Not one of the decisions relied upon by the Court of Appeals . . . comes close to establishing that the officers' conduct was unlawful."[11] The Court concluded its decision by declaring: "Neither the panel majority nor the respondent have identified a single precedent finding a Fourth Amendment violation under similar circumstances. The officers were thus entitled to qualified immunity."[12]

It is notable that both of these decisions were unanimous and that the justices saw them as sufficiently clear as to not even need briefing and oral argument. At the very least, they show that in police excessive force cases, the Court insists that there be a case with very similar facts or the officers must be deemed to be protected by qualified immunity. There thus is a high hurdle for plaintiffs seeking to recover for claims of excessive use of force by the police.

This surely disappoints those who believed that the Court might shift its approach to qualified immunity after the protests against police violence following the death of George Floyd and in the face of significant criticism of its jurisprudence in this area. Because qualified immunity is based on the Court's interpretation of a statute, Section 1983, Congress could change this law. The House of Representatives, in both 2020 and 2021, passed the George Floyd Justice in Policing Act that, among other things, would change the standard for qualified immunity. So far, though, it has been blocked in the Senate, and passage seems unlikely in the foreseeable future.

## *Bivens* Suits

The federal government has sovereign immunity and cannot be sued for money damages unless there is a federal statute expressly authorizing suit. No such statute exists to allow the federal government to be sued for constitutional violations. Typically, the only recourse for a person whose rights have been violated is to sue the federal officer who caused the harm.

Although a federal statute authorizes suits against state and local officials who violate the Constitution, no law exists to permit federal officials to be sued. In 1971, in the landmark case *Bivens vs. Six Unknown Named Agents of the Federal Bureau of Narcotics*, the Supreme Court held that federal officials who violate the Constitution can be sued for money damages notwithstanding the absence of a statute expressly permitting this action.[13]

In that case, agents of the narcotics bureau went into Webster Bivens' house without a warrant and subjected him to a humiliating search that clearly violated the Fourth Amendment. The Court ruled that Bivens could sue the agents who violated his rights for money damages. Subsequently, the Court determined that such suits against federal officers could be brought when officers engage in unconstitutional discrimination or impose cruel and unusual punishment.[14]

But since 1980, the Court has repeatedly restricted the availability of *Bivens*.[15] In fact, every Supreme Court decision in the past forty years regarding *Bivens* suits has ruled against their availability. In *Ziglar v. Abassi*, in 2017, the Court "made clear that expanding the *Bivens* remedy is now a 'disfavored' judicial activity" and that it would hesitate to extend *Bivens* to new contexts.[16]

The Court's decision in *Egbert vs. Boule* further limits this right to sue—this time for Fourth Amendment violations for illegal searches and seizures.[17] Robert Boule owns a bed-and-breakfast called The Smuggler's Inn in Blaine, Washington, near the Canadian border. Erik Egbert, a U.S. Border Patrol Agent, followed Boule and a passenger in his car to the inn. According to Boule's complaint, Boule asked Egbert to leave, but Egbert refused, became violent, and threw Boule to the ground. Egbert then checked the immigration paperwork for Boule's guest and left after finding nothing illegal.

Boule filed a grievance against Egbert with the border patrol. Boule alleges that Egbert then retaliated by contacting the Internal Revenue Service and state agencies, prompting an investigation and audit of Boule's tax returns. Boule sued Egbert for excessive force in violation of the Fourth Amendment and for violating the First Amendment by retaliating against him for his complaint.

The Court of Appeals for the Ninth Circuit held that these allegations were sufficient to allow Boule to sue. But Justice Clarence Thomas, writing for the majority in the 6–3 opinion, said that Bivens suits are "a disfavored judicial activity."[18] As such, he wrote, these suits should not be allowed at all in the border policing context. The Court concluded that it would be an extension of *Bivens* to allow suits against border agents or for retaliation, and such an extension would be undesirable.

The Court reformulated the test for when *Bivens* suits are available. The Court said,

> *First, we ask whether the case presents "a new* Bivens *context" —i.e., is it "meaningful[ly]" different from the three cases in which the Court has implied a damages action. Second, if a claim arises in a new context, a* Bivens *remedy is unavailable if there are "special factors" indicating that the Judiciary is at least arguably less equipped than Congress to "weigh the costs and benefits of allowing a damages action to proceed."* If there is even a single "reason to pause before applying *Bivens* in a new context," a court may not recognize a *Bivens* remedy.[19]

This decision further shields border agents who commit grievous harms from accountability to the victims of their actions. Just two years before, the Court held that a border agent in the United States could not be sued when he fired his gun across the Mexican border and killed a teenage boy who was playing on the other side.[20]

But, of course, the implications transcend the border context. The Court's refusal to allow federal officers to be sued for money damages means there will be no remedy for people whose rights have been violated. Money damages are essential to compensate injured victims and to deter wrongdoing. As Justice Sonia Sotomayor wrote in dissent, the Court's decision "will strip many more individuals who suffer injuries at the hands of other federal officers, and whose circumstances are materially indistinguishable from those in Bivens, of an important remedy."[21]

But as Justice Gorsuch noted in a separate opinion, Congress can easily fix this problem.[22] It could pass a statute—like the one authorizing suits against state and local officials—that expressly permits federal officers to be sued when they violate the Constitution. However, like a statute to fix qualified immunity, it seems unlikely such a bill will pass Congress in the foreseeable future.

## *Vega v. Tekoh*

In *Miranda v. Arizona* in 1966, the Supreme Court held that in-custodial police interrogation is inherently coercive.[23] The Court ruled to protect the privilege against self-incrimination; police are required to administer warnings before questioning a person in custody.

In 2000, the Supreme Court had the opportunity to reconsider its *Miranda* ruling and, in a 7–2 decision, emphatically reaffirmed it. *United States v. Dickerson* arose in an unusual procedural context.[24] In 1968, two years after *Miranda*, Congress adopted a statute that provided that confessions shall be admissible as evidence in federal court, notwithstanding the failure to properly administer warnings, as long as the confession was voluntary. From the Nixon administration through the Clinton presidency, every Justice Department, whether under a Democratic or a Republican president, refused to invoke this statute because of a belief that it was unconstitutional.

In *Dickerson*, a confession was excluded by the federal district court for failure to properly administer *Miranda* warnings. The government appealed. The U.S. Court of Appeals for the Fourth Circuit, on its own, raised §3501, asked for briefing as to its constitutionality, upheld the law, and held the confession was admissible because it was voluntary. The Supreme Court granted certiorari and reconsidered *Miranda* and its constitutional status. The Court reaffirmed *Miranda* and declared it a constitutional requirement that Congress could not eliminate by statute. In an opinion by Chief Justice William Rehnquist, the Court declared, "We hold that *Miranda*, being a constitutional decision of this Court, may not be in effect overruled by an Act of Congress, and we decline to overrule *Miranda* ourselves. We therefore hold that *Miranda* and its progeny in this Court govern the admissibility of statements made during custodial interrogation in both state and federal courts."[25]

The usual remedy for a violation of *Miranda* is the exclusion of the statements that were gained without proper warnings. But could an individual interrogated without warnings bring a civil suit for money damages? In *Chavez v. Martinez*, in 2003, the Court held that civil suits are not possible if the statements are not introduced into evidence against the suspect.[26] But what if the statements are introduced? That was the issue this term in *Vega v. Tekoh,* and the Court, in a 6–3 decision, held that civil suits for money damages are not permissible for *Miranda* violations, even when the statements are admitted at trial against the defendant.[27]

Terrence Tekoh was working as a certified nursing assistant at a Los Angeles medical center. When a female patient accused him of touching her inappropriately, the police were called and Los Angeles County Sheriff's Deputy Carlos Vega responded.

Vega took Tekoh into a small room and questioned him at length in an aggressive manner. After extensive and intimidating questioning, Tekoh provided a written statement apologizing for inappropriately touching the patient's genitals. Although Tekoh seems to have been unquestionably in custody, in that a reasonable person under these circumstances would not have felt free to leave under the circumstances, Vega never administered *Miranda* warnings.

Tekoh was arrested and charged in California state court with unlawful sexual penetration. Tekoh was tried and acquitted. Tekoh then brought this action under 42 U.S.C. § 1983 against Vega and several other defendants seeking damages for alleged violations of his constitutional rights, including his Fifth Amendment right against compelled self-incrimination.

The issue was whether there could be a civil suit for money damages against a police officer for violating the Fifth Amendment by failing to administer *Miranda* warnings.

The Court, in a 6–3 decision split along ideological lines, ruled that no such suits are permissible. Justice Samuel Alito wrote the opinion for the Court. He said that *Miranda* does not create a constitutional right, but instead, "[s]ince *Miranda*, the Court has repeatedly described the rules it adopted as "prophylactic."[28]

The Court held that *Dickerson* did not change this understanding, despite some language to the contrary in Chief Justice Rehnquist's majority opinion. The Court said, "Subsequent cases confirm that *Dickerson* did not upend the Court's understanding of the *Miranda* rules as prophylactic. In sum, a violation of *Miranda* does not necessarily constitute a violation of the Constitution, and therefore such a violation does not constitute 'the deprivation of [a] right . . . secured by the Constitution.'"[29]

Justice Elena Kagan wrote for the dissent. She said, "The Court's decision in *Miranda v. Arizona* (1966) affords well-known protections to suspects who are interrogated by police while in custody. Those protections derive from the Constitution."[30] The dissent saw *Miranda* as creating a Fifth Amendment right for those questioned in custody to be given the required warnings. Sharply disagreeing with the majority, she said that

> Dickerson v. United States *tells us in no uncertain terms that* Miranda *is a "constitutional rule." And that rule grants a corresponding right: If police fail to provide the* Miranda *warnings to a suspect before interrogating him, then he is generally entitled to have any resulting confession excluded from his trial. From those facts, only one conclusion can follow—that* Miranda*'s protections are a "right[ ]" "secured by the Constitution" under the federal civil rights statute.*[31]

Justice Kagan was especially concerned about how those, like Tekoh, whose Fifth Amendment rights have been violated, are left with no remedy.

Also, if *Miranda* is not a constitutional right, must state courts continue to follow it and might the Supreme Court reconsider allowing *Miranda* violations to be raised on habeas corpus?

## *Thompson v. Clark*

The one victory for a civil rights plaintiff was in *Thompson v. Clark*.[32] Larry Thompson and his wife lived with their newborn baby in an apartment in Brooklyn, New York. Thompson's sister-in-law, who had a history of mental illness, was staying with them. She called 911 and said she thought the baby was being sexually abused.

Two emergency medical technicians (EMTs) came to the apartment, but Thompson denied that anyone had called 911. The EMTs left and informed the police of the situation. The EMTs and four police officers then returned to the apartment. When they arrived, Thompson told them they could not come in without a warrant. The police officers nonetheless entered and handcuffed Thompson after a brief scuffle. The EMTs took the baby to the hospital for evaluation. The redness was a case of diaper rash. The medical professionals found no signs of abuse.

Meanwhile, the police officers arrested Thompson for resisting their entry into the apartment. Thompson was taken to a local hospital and then to jail. While Thompson was in custody, one of the police officers prepared and filed a criminal complaint charging Thompson with obstructing governmental administration and resisting arrest. Thompson remained in custody for two days.

Before trial, the prosecution moved to dismiss the charges, and the trial judge, in turn, dismissed the case. The prosecutor did not explain why she sought to dismiss the charges, nor did the trial judge explain why he dismissed the case.

After the criminal prosecution ended, Thompson brought suit for damages under 42 U.S.C. § 1983 against the police officers who had arrested and charged him. Thompson alleged several constitutional violations, including a Fourth Amendment claim for "malicious prosecution."

The federal district court dismissed Thompson's suit, saying that under Second Circuit precedent, Thompson had to show that his criminal prosecution ended not merely without a conviction, but also with some affirmative indication of his innocence. The Second Circuit affirmed.

The Supreme Court, in a 6–3 decision, reversed and ruled that a malicious prosecution claim does not require that the plaintiff show an affirmative indication of his or her actual innocence. Justice Brett Kavanaugh wrote for the Court and said that at common law, there were three requirements for a malicious prosecution claim. American courts described the elements of the malicious prosecution tort as follows: "(i) the suit or proceeding was 'instituted without any probable cause'; (ii) the 'motive in instituting' the suit 'was malicious,' which was often defined in this context as without probable cause and for a purpose other than bringing the defendant to justice; and (iii) the prosecution 'terminated in the acquittal or discharge of the accused.'"[33]

The Court found that these are the requirements for a malicious prosecution claim under the Fourth Amendment. The issue was whether proof of a favorable termination requires an affirmative indication of actual innocence. The Court said, "[t]o resolve that disagreement, we must look to American malicious prosecution tort law as of 1871."[34] This, too, is an example of the Court emphasizing history in determining the meaning of the Constitution today.

The Court looked at this history and concluded that showing a favorable termination does not require an affirmative indication of actual innocence. Of course, in the United States, there is generally no mechanism to receive this indication. When charges are dismissed, a court does not make a pronouncement that the defendant was actually innocent. The Court stated: "In sum, we hold that a Fourth Amendment claim under § 1983 for malicious prosecution does not require the plaintiff to show that the criminal prosecution ended with some affirmative indication of innocence. A plaintiff need only show that the criminal prosecution ended without a conviction. Thompson has satisfied that requirement here."[35]

In writing for the dissent, Justice Alito disagreed with allowing a Fourth Amendment claim for malicious prosecution. He objected, saying that the "Court's recognition of a Fourth Amendment malicious-prosecution claim has no basis in our precedents."[36]

## Conclusion

Overall, the civil rights cases fit the themes of October Term 2021. The conservative position generally prevailed, often by the same 6–3 margin seen in many of the high-profile cases of the term. In some of the cases, the Court followed a familiar pattern of decisions. The Court, like in many prior cases, used qualified immunity to deny recovery to individuals suing police officers for excessive force and denied recovery in a *Bivens* suit. These are areas where Congress could change the law by statute to provide recoveries for those whose constitutional rights have been violated, but such legislation seems unlikely for the foreseeable future.

## Endnotes

1. Harlow v. Fitzgerald, 457 U.S. 800 (1982).
2. 138 S. Ct. 577, 589 (2018).
3. *Id.* at 590 (internal citations omitted).
4. Zadeh v. Robinson, 902 F. 3d. 483, 498 (5th Cir. 2018)
5. *Id.* at 499.
6. 141 S. Ct. 52 (2000).
7. 142 S. Ct. 4 (2021).
8. *Id.* at 7.
9. *Id.* at 8.
10. 142 S. Ct. 9 (2021).
11. *Id.* at 11.
12. *Id.*
13. 403 U.S. 388 (1971).
14. Davis v. Passman, 442 U.S. 228 (1979) (*Bivens* suit can be brought for violation of equal protection under the due process clause of the Fifth Amendment); Carlson v. Green, 446 U.S. 14 (1980) (*Bivens* suit can be brought for violation of cruel and unusual punishment clause of the Eighth Amendment).
15. *See, e.g.,* Ziglar v. Abbasi, 137 S. Ct. 1843 (2017); Hui v. Castaneda, 555 U.S. 799 (2010); Wilkie v. Robbins, 551 U.S. 537 (2007); Correctional Services Corp. v. Malesko, 534 U.S. 61 (2001), all discussed below.
16. 137 S. Ct. 1843, 1857 (2017).
17. 142 S. Ct. 1793 (2022).
18. *Id.* at 1803.
19. *Id.* (emphasis added).

20. Hernandez v. Mesa, 140 S. Ct. 735 (2020).
21. 142 S. Ct. 1793, 1811 (Sotomayor, J., dissenting).
22. *Id.* at 1810 (Gorsuch, J., dissenting).
23. 384 U.S. 436 (1966).
24. 530 U.S. 428 (2000).
25. *Id.* at 432.
26. 538 U.S. 760 (2003).
27. 142 S. Ct. 2095 (2022).
28. *Id.* at 2102 (internal citations omitted).
29. *Id.* at 2106.
30. 142 S. Ct. at 2108 (Kagan, J., dissenting).
31. *Id.*
32. 142 S. Ct. 1332 (2022).
33. *Id.* at 1338.
34. *Id.*
35. *Id.* at 1341.
36. *Id.* at 1344 (Alito, J., dissenting).

5

# Criminal Law and Procedure

In a term of blockbuster cases where the conservative position prevailed, the criminal law and criminal procedure cases were more mixed in their results. There were two important Sixth Amendment cases, one where the criminal defendant prevailed and one where the government won. There were several cases involving federal criminal statutes where the criminal defendant triumphed in the Supreme Court. But the Court moved the law further to the right in the area of habeas corpus and suggested even more dramatic changes to come.[1]

## Sixth Amendment

There were two cases concerning Sixth Amendment rights. *United States v. Tsarnaev* was an important case strongly affirming the discretion of trial judges, especially in high-profile cases.[2] Dzhokhar Tsarnaev and his brother Tamerlin were responsible for the bombing at the Boston Marathon in 2013 that killed three people and injured hundreds of others. Tamerlin was killed by the police in a shoot-out, but Dzhokhar was arrested and tried for murder in federal court.

Dzhokhar's lawyer asked for a change of venue in light of all of the publicity surrounding the case and how many people in Boston were directly or indirectly affected by the bombing. The judge refused and said that care would be taken during voir dire to select an unbiased jury. The defense wanted the judge to ask prospective jurors about what they had seen and heard and knew about the case. The judge instead asked prospective jurors if they had formed an opinion and if they could be unbiased.

Voir dire took 21 days and the defense four times moved to change venue, with all of the requests being denied. Dzhokhar was convicted. At the penalty phase, the defense wanted to introduce evidence of a triple murder committed by Tamerlin. The defense theory was that Dzokhar was under the influence of his older brother and that this was a mitigating circumstance against the imposition of the death penalty. The judge refused to allow the evidence of the other murder, expressing concern that it would cause a trial within a trial and be a distraction for the jury. The jury recommended a death sentence, which the judge imposed.

The U.S. Court of Appeals for the First Circuit reversed the death sentence on the ground that the judge had not done enough to ensure an unbiased jury. The Court of Appeals also reversed based on the trial judge's failure to allow the jury to hear evidence in the penalty phase as to a murder that Tamerlin had committed previously.

The Supreme Court, in a 6–3 decision, reversed the First Circuit and ruled in favor of the government. Justice Thomas wrote the majority opinion and as to both issues stressed the discretion of the trial judge. As for the first issue on jury selection, the Court emphasized the discretion of trial courts, especially in high-profile cases, to decide how to conduct voir dire. The Court stated:

> *We have repeatedly said that jury selection falls "particularly within the province of the trial judge." That is so because a trial "judge's appraisal is ordinarily influenced by a host of factors impossible to capture fully in the record," such as a "prospective juror's inflection, sincerity, demeanor, candor, body language, and apprehension of duty." A trial court's broad discretion in*

*this area includes deciding what questions to ask prospective jurors. The court of appeals reviews the district court's questioning of prospective jurors only for abuse of discretion. That discretion does not vanish when a case garners public attention. Indeed, "[w]hen pretrial publicity is at issue, 'primary reliance on the judgment of the trial court makes [especially] good sense.'"*[3]

The Court concluded that the federal judge did not abuse his discretion in jury selection and rejected that courts of appeals have supervisory power that allows them to second guess the trial court as to how to conduct jury selection.

Likewise, as to the second issue, the Court spoke broadly of the trial court's discretion to decide what evidence to allow in at the penalty phase of a capital trial. The Court rejected the argument that the Federal Death Penalty Act required that the judge admit the evidence. Justice Thomas wrote:

*The District Court acknowledged Dzhokhar's rationale but excluded the evidence because it was "without any probative value" and "would be confusing to the jury." That conclusion was reasonable and not an abuse of the District Court's discretion. Dzhokhar sought to divert the sentencing jury's attention to a triple homicide that Tamerlin allegedly committed years prior, though there was no allegation that Dzhokhar had any role in that crime. Nor was there any way to confirm or verify the relevant facts, since all of the parties involved were dead.*[4]

Justice Breyer wrote for the three dissenting justices and focused on the second issue. He argued that the Federal Death Penalty Act broadly allows defendants in capital cases to present all evidence. The dissenters agreed with the First Circuit that the trial judge abused his discretion in not allowing the defense to raise the theory and present the evidence it wanted. Justice Breyer said: "I conclude, then, that the reasons the District Court gave do not justify excluding the Waltham murder evidence, and it was an abuse of discretion to do so. Nor was the exclusion harmless."[5]

The other Sixth Amendment case involved the Confrontation Clause of the Sixth Amendment. In *Crawford v. Washington*, in 2004, the Court significantly changed the law concerning the Confrontation Clause.[6] The Court held that prosecutors may not use testimonial statements from unavailable witnesses, even if they are reliable.

What, though, if a criminal defendant uses a statement from an unavailable witness; may the prosecution then use other parts of that statement? That was the issue in *Hemphill v. New York*.[7]

The case arose from tragic facts: In 2006, a stray 9-millimeter bullet killed a two-year-old child in the Bronx. The State charged Nicholas Morris with the murder, but after the trial commenced, it offered him a plea deal for a lesser charge. The State specifically required Morris to admit to a new charge of possession of a .357-magnum revolver, not the 9-millimeter handgun originally charged in the indictment and used in the killing.

Several years later, the State prosecuted Darrell Hemphill for the same murder. At his trial, Hemphill blamed Morris, and he elicited undisputed testimony from a prosecution witness that police had recovered 9-millimeter ammunition from Morris's nightstand. Morris was outside the United States and not available to testify. Hemphill, as part of his presentation, relied on statements from Morris's plea allocution.

The State then wanted to use other parts of the transcript of Morris's plea allocution as evidence to rebut Hemphill's theory that Morris committed the murder. The Court allowed this and reasoned that Hemphill's arguments and evidence had "open[ed] the door" to the introduction of these testimonial out-of-court statements, not subjected to cross-examination, because they were 'reasonably necessary' to 'correct' the 'misleading impression' Hemphill had created."[8]

The question was whether the trial court, in allowing the prosecutor to quote from the plea allocution, violated Hemphill's Sixth Amendment right to confront the witnesses against him. The Court held that it did. Justice Sotomayor wrote for the Court in an 8–1 decision and concluded: "Hemphill did not forfeit his confrontation right merely by making the plea allocution arguably relevant to his theory of defense."[9]

The Court stressed that under *Crawford*, Hemphill's Sixth Amendment rights were violated in the trial court admitting the testimony from the unavailable witness. The Court stated: "The upshot is that the role of the trial judge is not, for Confrontation Clause purposes, to weigh the reliability or credibility of testimonial hearsay evidence; it is to ensure that the Constitution's procedures for testing the reliability of that evidence are followed. The trial court here violated this principle by admitting unconfronted, testimonial hearsay against Hemphill simply because the judge deemed his presentation to have created a misleading impression that the testimonial hearsay was reasonably necessary to correct." Justice Sotomayor was clear that the trial judge violated the Sixth Amendment: "For Confrontation Clause purposes, it was not for the judge to determine whether Hemphill's theory that Morris was the shooter was unreliable, incredible, or otherwise misleading in light of the State's proffered, unconfronted plea evidence. Nor, under the Clause, was it the judge's role to decide that this evidence was reasonably necessary to correct that misleading impression. Such inquiries are antithetical to the Confrontation Clause."

The case is thus a strong reaffirmation of *Crawford v. Washington* and its exclusion from trials of testimonial statements from unavailable witnesses.

## Federal Criminal Statutes

There were a few important cases concerning federal criminal statutes. In *Wooden v. United States*, the Court considered when crimes are committed on separate occasions for purposes of the Armed Career Criminal Act.[10] In the course of one evening, William Dale Wooden burglarized 10 units in a single storage facility. He later pleaded guilty to 10 counts of burglary, one for each storage unit he had entered that night. Some two decades later, a federal district court concluded that those convictions were enough to subject Wooden to enhanced criminal penalties under the Armed Career Criminal Act (ACCA). That statute mandates a 15-year minimum sentence for unlawful gun possession when the offender has three or more prior convictions for violent felonies like burglary "committed on occasions different from one another."

The Court, in an opinion by Justice Elena Kagan, held that William Dale Wooden's 10 burglary offenses arising from a single criminal episode did not occur on different "occasions" and thus count as only one prior conviction under the Armed Career Criminal Act. She explained:

> *Here, every relevant consideration shows that Wooden burglarized ten storage units on a single occasion, even though his criminal activity resulted in double-digit convictions. Wooden committed his burglaries on a single night, in a single uninterrupted course of conduct. The crimes all took place at one location, a one-building storage facility with one address. Each offense was essentially identical, and all were intertwined with the others. The burglaries were part and parcel of the same scheme, actuated by the same motive, and accomplished by the same means. Indeed, each burglary in some sense facilitated the next, as Wooden moved from unit to unit to unit, all in a row.*[11]

It is an issue that arises in many contexts. In a bar fight, is each punch a separate battery? In an illegal poker game, is each hand a separate crime? Justice Kagan's opinion is limited to the context of the Armed Career Criminal Act, but it is an important clarification as to this significant federal statute.

*Ruan v. United States* involved when a doctor can be convicted under the Controlled Substances Act for prescriptions of drugs covered by the statute.[12] A provision of the Controlled Substances Act, makes it a federal crime, "[e]xcept as authorized[,] . . . for any person knowingly or intentionally . . . to manufacture, distribute, or dispense . . . a controlled substance," such as opioids. Registered doctors may prescribe these substances to their patients. But, as provided by regulation, a prescription is only authorized when a doctor issues it "for a legitimate medical purpose . . . acting in the usual course of his professional practice."

Two doctors were convicted under the statute for dispensing controlled substances not "as authorized." The issue was what *mens rea* is required for a conviction under the statute. The Court, in an opinion by Justice Stephen Breyer, declared: "We hold that the statute's 'knowingly or intentionally' mens rea applies to authorization. After a defendant produces evidence that he or she was authorized to dispense controlled substances, the Government must prove beyond a reasonable doubt that the defendant knew that he or she was acting in an unauthorized manner, or intended to do so."[13]

Finally, *Concepcion v. United States* involved the First Step Act.[14] Congress passed the Fair Sentencing Act of 2010 to correct the wide disparity between crack and powder cocaine sentencing. Section 2 of that Act increased the amount of crack cocaine needed to trigger a 5-to-40-year sentencing range from 5 grams to 28 grams. The Fair Sentencing Act did not apply retroactively, but in 2011, the Sentencing Commission amended the Sentencing Guidelines to lower the Guidelines range for crack cocaine offenses and applied that reduction retroactively for some defendants. In 2018, Congress enacted the First Step Act, authorizing district courts to "impose a reduced sentence" on defendants serving sentences for certain crack cocaine offenses "as if sections 2 and 3 of the Fair Sentencing Act . . . were in effect at the time the covered offense was committed."

Carlos Concepcion pleaded guilty to one count of distributing five or more grams of crack cocaine was sentenced in 2009 to 19 years (228 months) in prison. Concepcion later sought resentencing under the First Step Act. He argued that he would no longer be considered a career offender because one of his prior convictions had been vacated and his remaining convictions would not constitute crimes of violence that trigger the enhancement. Also, Concepcion pointed to post-sentencing evidence of rehabilitation.

The issue before the Court was whether, when deciding if it should "impose a reduced sentence" on an individual under the First Step Act of 2018, a district court must or may consider intervening legal and factual developments. The Court, in a 5–4 decision, held that district courts may do this. Justice Sonia Sotomayor wrote the majority opinion, joined by Justices Thomas, Breyer, Kagan, and Gorsuch.

The Court emphasized the inherent discretion of courts in sentencing. The Court declared:

> *It is only when Congress or the Constitution limits the scope of information that a district court may consider in deciding whether, and to what extent, to modify a sentence, that a district court's discretion to consider information is restrained. Nothing in the First Step Act contains such a limitation. Because district courts are always obligated to consider nonfrivolous arguments presented by the parties, the First Step Act requires district courts to consider intervening changes when parties raise them. By its terms, however, the First Step Act does not*

> *compel courts to exercise their discretion to reduce any sentence based on those arguments.*[15]

## Habeas Corpus

Over the last half century, the Supreme Court and Congress have significantly restricted the availability of habeas corpus. While the Warren Court expanded the ability of those convicted in state court to raise constitutional issues in federal court on habeas corpus, ever since the Court has created numerous restrictions. These have included imposing strict exhaustion requirements, limiting habeas corpus to already existing constitutional rights, preventing Fourth Amendment claims from being relitigated on habeas corpus, and precluding raising issues that were not litigated in state court.

In 1996, Congress went even further in the Anti-Terrorism and Effective Death Penalty Act (AEDPA) in greatly limiting habeas corpus. It imposed a one-year statute of limitations on habeas petitions, limited a prisoner to one petition challenging a conviction, and created a restrictive standard for when habeas petitions can be granted. For the last quarter of a century, the Supreme Court has consistently interpreted this statute to make it ever harder for a habeas petition to be granted.

The Warren Court was animated by the vision that habeas corpus should be available to those who claim that they were convicted or sentenced in violation of the Constitution. But its more conservative successors and Congress have questioned the need for habeas corpus once someone has had the chance to litigate their claims in state court and have great concern that it lets guilty people go free.

Two recent Supreme Court decisions, both not surprisingly 6–3 rulings divided along ideological lines, impose new restrictions on habeas corpus. And one of them suggests that the Court might go even further in limiting habeas corpus. Indeed, if Justice Gorsuch's reasoning in *Brown v. Davenport* is followed, it will almost completely eliminate the ability of those convicted to ever bring a habeas corpus petition.[16]

The Supreme Court has held that the Sixth Amendment right to an attorney includes a right to effective assistance of counsel. But studies show, and observation confirms, that many criminal defendants have grossly deficient representation. Some states, though, preclude claims of ineffective assistance of counsel from being raised on direct appeal. The first time they can be presented in state court is on a motion for post-conviction relief, such as a habeas petition brought in state court under state law.

What, though, if the attorney fails to properly raise the claim of ineffective assistance of counsel in the state post-conviction proceeding? Is the failure to raise this a procedural default that bars the claim from being raised in a federal habeas corpus petition? If so, then a person convicted even with egregiously deficient representation never would have the chance for it to be heard in federal court.

In *Martinez v. Ryan* (2012), the Court came to the common-sense conclusion that ineffective assistance of counsel claims can be raised on federal habeas corpus if they could not have been raised in state court on direct appeal and if they were not presented in a state post-conviction proceeding.[17] But what if the federal court in such a situation needs to hold an evidentiary hearing to determine whether there was ineffective assistance of counsel? In *Shinn v. Ramirez*, the Court held that this generally is not possible; the federal court must rely solely on the evidentiary record from the state court proceeding.

*Shinn v. Martinez Ramirez*, decided on May 22, involved two defendants who had been convicted of murder in Arizona state court.[18] Arizona does not allow ineffective assistance of counsel claims to be raised on direct appeal. In these cases, it was not raised in Arizona court in post-conviction proceedings. Both defendants sought to raise the claims in federal court on habeas corpus based on *Martinez v. Ryan*. In each instance, the federal district court allowed the habeas petitioner to present additional evidence to support the claim of ineffective assistance of counsel. In one of the cases, the new evidence showed a likelihood that the defendant was actually innocent and had been wrongly convicted and sentenced to death.

But the Supreme Court, in an opinion by Justice Clarence Thomas, ruled that holding the hearings was impermissible. Justice Thomas began by saying that "the availability of habeas relief is narrowly circumscribed."[19] He said that habeas corpus "intrudes on state sovereignty" by allowing guilty people to go free and it "imposes significant costs on state criminal justice systems."[20]

The Court focused on a provision adopted as part of the Antiterrorism and Effective Death Penalty Act, 28 U.S.C. §2254(e)(2), which greatly limits the ability of federal courts to hold evidentiary hearings on habeas corpus. The Court said this applies even when there is a claim of ineffective assistance of counsel that could not have been raised earlier. The federal court is confined to the state court record and cannot consider additional evidence, even when it may show, as in one of the cases before it, that the defendant is innocent of the crime for which he was sentenced to death.

Justice Sonia Sotomayor wrote a strenuous dissent, joined by Justices Stephen Breyer and Elena Kagan.[21] She said that this "all but overrules" *Martinez v. Ryan* because almost always there will be a need for additional evidence to show ineffective assistance of counsel. She lamented that the Court "makes illusory the protections of the 6th Amendment." She wrote: "The Court's decision will leave many people who were convicted in violation of the Sixth Amendment to face incarceration or even execution without any meaningful chance to vindicate their right to counsel."[22]

The other habeas case was *Brown v. Davenport*.[23] Ervine Davenport was tried for murder in Michigan. During his trial, he was shackled at his hands, waist, and ankles. It is unclear whether this was visible to the jury. In *Deck v. Missouri* (2005), the Court held that the due process forbids shackling a criminal defendant at trial absent "a special need."[24] On habeas corpus, Davenport argued that his conviction violated due process because there was no finding of a special need by the trial court.

In *Brecht v. Abrahamson* (1993), the Court held that a state prisoner seeking to challenge his conviction on federal habeas corpus must show that the error had a "substantial and injurious effect or influence" on the outcome of his trial.[25] The issue in *Brown v. Davenport* was whether this is sufficient or whether the habeas petitioner must also meet the requirement created in the Anti-Terrorism and Effective Death Penalty Act, 28 U.S.C. §2254(d) and demonstrate that the conviction was (1) "contrary to" or an "unreasonable application of " clearly established federal law, as determined by the decisions of this Court, or (2) based on an "unreasonable determination of the facts" presented in the state-court proceeding.

In *Brown v. Davenport*, the Court concluded that a habeas petitioner must meet *both* the standard for harmful error from *Brecht v. Abrahamson* and the requirements of Section 2254(d). Justice Gorsuch, writing for a 6–3 majority, went beyond that and suggested that habeas corpus should be available only in instances where the Court lacked the jurisdiction to try the defendant. Justice Gorsuch said that historically, "[u]sually, a prisoner could not use it to challenge a final judgment of conviction issued by a court of competent jurisdiction."[26]

Justice Gorsuch noted that in *Brown v. Allen* (1953), the Court changed the law to allow a person convicted in state court to relitigate constitutional claims in federal habeas corpus.[27] As he did a year earlier in a concurrence in *Edwards v. Vannoy* (2021), Justice Gorsuch implied that *Brown v. Allen* was wrongly decided.[28] Here, though, five justices join him. Perhaps this is just part of explaining why the Court is being restrictive and requiring that both the *Brecht v. Abrahamson* standard for harmful error and the Section 2254(d) requirements be met. Or perhaps this portends an even more dramatic change in habeas corpus law in the future.

If habeas corpus in federal court is limited to arguing that the trial court lacked jurisdiction, it will be effectively eliminated. This is especially what concerned the dissenting justices. Justice Kagan wrote a dissent, joined by Justices Breyer and Sotomayor. Justice Kagan declared: "Because the majority begins with some law-chambers history, I do too—though fair warning: My discussion is no more relevant than the majority's to the issue before us. . . . [T]he majority, unprompted, embarks on that project, perhaps hoping that the seeds it sows now will yield more succulent fruit in cases to come."[29] She said that Justice Gorsuch's "theory, in its fundamentals is wrong. Federal courts long before Brown extended habeas relief to prisoners held in violation of the Constitution—even after a final conviction." She reviewed the history of habeas corpus and said that, "[c]ontrary to the majority, then, our decision in *Brown* built on decades and decades of history."[30]

The dissent also argued that, based on precedents and statutory interpretation, once harmful error was shown under *Brecht*, there should be no need to meet the requirements imposed by the Anti-Terrorism and Effective Death Penalty Act.

These two cases reveal profoundly differing views of the role of habeas corpus. The conservative justices seek to significantly limit it, by judicially created doctrines and by enforcing the restrictions created by Congress in AEDPA. They see it as an affront to state courts and as a vehicle for dangerous, guilty people to go free. By contrast, the liberal justices see habeas corpus as an essential way to make sure that no one is imprisoned or executed in violation of the Constitution. They want the federal courts to be available to redress constitutional violations. These two 6–3 decisions reflect exactly that division on the current Court. And *Brown* suggests that there may be further, dramatic restrictions on habeas corpus to come from the Roberts Court.

## Endnotes

1. The Court also decided a case about the Fifth Amendment, *Vega v. Tekoh*, 142 S. Ct. 2095 (2022), which concerned whether a civil suit for money damages could be brought for failure to administer *Miranda* warnings. Because this involved the availability of a damages remedy under 42 U.S.C. § 1983, it is covered in Chapter 4 on Civil Rights Litigation.
2. United States v. Tsarnaev, U.S.142 S. Ct. 1024 (2022).
3. *Id.* at 1034.
4. *Id.* at 1037.
5. *Id.* at 1050 (Breyer, J., dissenting).
6. 541 U.S. 36 (2004).
7. 142 S. Ct. 681 (2022).
8. *Id.* at 686.
9. *Id.*
10. 142 S. Ct. 1063 (2022).
11. *Id.* at 1071.
12. 142 S. Ct. 2370 (2022).
13. *Id.* at 2375.
14. 142 S. Ct. 2389 (2022).
15. *Id.* at 2396.
16. 142 S. Ct. 1510 (2022).
17. 132 S. Ct. 1309 (2012).
18. 142 S. Ct. 1718 (2022).

19. *Id.* at 1736.
20. *Id.* at 1724.
21. *Id.* at 1740 (Sotomayor, J., dissenting).
22. *Id.* at 1750.
23. *See* 142 S. Ct. 1510 (2022).
24. 544 U.S. 622, 626 (2005).
25. 507 U.S. 619, 623 (1993).
26. 142 S. Ct. 1510 at 1520.
27. *See* 344 U.S. 443 (1953).
28. *See generally* 141 S. Ct. 1547 (2021).
29. 142 S. Ct. 1510 at 1531 (Kagan, J., dissenting).
30. *Id.* at 1534.

# 6

# Elections

The "shadow docket" refers to orders and opinions that the Court issues when there are requests for emergency rulings. Throughout American history, litigants have gone to the Supreme Court for such orders. For example, in death penalty cases, there often have been requests for emergency stays of execution. But as others have documented in recent years, there has been a dramatic rise in important matters being resolved on the shadow docket.[1]

This term, there were no major decisions about election law after briefing and oral argument. But there were some orders in election cases that could have important implications for the future.

## *Merrill v. Milligan*

The Supreme Court's ruling in *Merrill v. Milligan*, on Monday, February 7, will make it harder for federal courts to enjoin illegal voting practices.[2] A three-judge federal district court—which included two judges appointed by President Donald Trump and one appointed by President Bill Clinton—found that the congressional districts drawn by the Alabama legislature likely violated the Voting Rights Act.[3] But the Supreme Court, in a 5–4 ruling, with Chief Justice John Roberts joining the three liberal justices in dissent, stayed the lower court ruling and allowed the discriminatory Alabama map to be used in the 2022 elections.

The three-judge federal court in Alabama heard seven days of testimony, read over 1,000 pages of briefing, and concluded that the map drawn by the Alabama legislature for congressional seats violated Section 2 of the Voting Rights Act. This provision prohibits state and local governments from having election systems that discriminate against minority voters. None of the nine justices disagreed with the lower court's conclusion about the discriminatory effect of the Alabama legislature's districting. Justice Elena Kagan, in her dissent, explained, "Alabama's population is 27% Black, but under the plan, Black voters have the power to elect their preferred candidates in only one of the State's seven congressional districts."[4]

One of the most basic rules of appellate procedure is that a stay of a lower court decision should be granted only if there is a substantial likelihood that the appellant will prevail on the merits. This, of course, is a general requirement for any form of equitable relief. Yet here, none of the five conservative justices pointed to any error of law or fact by the three-judge district court. Nor did any of the justices claim that the three-judge federal court misapplied the law in finding a violation of the Voting Rights Act. As Chief Justice Roberts explained in his dissent, "the District Court properly applied existing law in an extensive opinion with no apparent errors for our correction."[5]

Why, then, did the conservative justices stay the ruling by the three-judge court? There was no opinion of the Court, but Justice Kavanaugh, who was in the majority, wrote an opinion explaining the rationale behind the stay. He invoked the principle that federal courts should not issue changes to state and local election practices soon before an election. He wrote: "The stay order follows this Court's election-law precedents, which establish (i) that federal district courts ordinarily should not enjoin state election laws in the period close to an election, and (ii) that federal appellate courts should stay injunctions when, as here, lower federal courts contravene that principle. See, e.g., *Purcell v. Gonzalez*, 549 U. S. 1 (2006) (per curiam)."[6]

*Purcell v. Gonzalez* also was a Supreme Court order, handed down without briefing or oral argument. The issue in *Purcell* was whether the Court should stay an order by the Ninth Circuit to enjoin an Arizona law that required proof of identification for voting. The district court had found that the plaintiffs failed to show "a strong likelihood" of prevailing on the merits, but the Ninth Circuit reversed.[7] The Supreme Court said, "Given the imminence of the election and the inadequate time to resolve the factual disputes, our action today shall of necessity allow the election to proceed without an injunction suspending the voter identification rules."[8]

The Court has invoked *Purcell v. Gonzalez* many times in the last 15 years as establishing that federal courts should not enjoin state and local election practices soon before an election. For example, in *Republican National Committee v. Democratic National Committee* (2020), a federal district court in Wisconsin issued an order, five days before the scheduled election, that absentee ballots mailed and postmarked after election day, April 7, still would be counted so long as they were received by April 13.[9] The judge did this because of the dramatic increase in absentee ballots in April 2020 at the height of concern over the COVID-19 pandemic. Wisconsin law had previously required that they be received by election day.[10]

The Court said that "[e]xtending the date by which ballots may be cast by voters—not just received by the municipal clerks but cast by voters—for an additional six days after the scheduled election day fundamentally alters the nature of the election."[11] The Court invoked *Purcell v. Gonzalez* and said, "This Court has repeatedly emphasized that lower federal courts should ordinarily not alter the election rules on the eve of an election."[12]

The Court has never explained what is sufficiently close to the election to justify the application of *Purcell*. The Alabama case was not a situation where the federal court was acting days or even weeks before the election. The federal district court issued its order in February, but the Alabama primary was not until May and the general election is not until November.

Moreover, Justice Kavanaugh's approach would make challenges to election districting almost impossible for the first election after districts are drawn. New districts are not drawn until after the census, and litigation then takes time. If a legislature just delays districting long enough, then no federal court can hear a challenge in time before the next election. Under Justice Kavanaugh's reasoning, if Alabama drew districts that would have made it unlikely that any Black representative could have been elected, then there still could have been no relief from the federal court before the election.

Justice Kavanaugh stressed that the Court was not ruling on the merits. But its action does not preserve the status quo since the maps from prior elections are not being used. Instead, it puts in place an electoral map that a three-judge federal court found to be discriminatory. The result of the ruling is that the map drawn by the Alabama legislature which lessens the voting strength of Blacks, in violation of the Voting Rights Act, will be used in the 2022 primary and general election, as the Supreme Court will not hear this case until the fall of 2022 and likely not decide until 2023. The almost certain result, which no one disputes, is an additional Republican seat in the House of Representatives.

The Court granted certiorari in *Merrill v. Milligan* and will hear it next term. But its use of the *Purcell* principle to limit federal judicial power is quite significant in itself.

On June 28, the Court took a similar action with regard to districting in Louisiana.[13] A federal district court found that the districting in Louisiana for seats in the House of Representatives likely violated the Voting Rights Act by diluting Black voting strength and ordered the creation of a second majority Black congressional district in Louisiana.[14] The Supreme Court, in a 6–3 decision split along ideological lines, stayed the judge's order imposing the new districts until it hears *Merrill v. Milligan* next term.

The result, as with Alabama, is that the Supreme Court's order means that midterm elections in Louisiana will take place this year using maps that a lower court found are likely to hurt the power of Black voters.

## *Wisconsin State Legislature v. Wisconsin Elections Commission*

Another important voting matter on the shadow docket arose in Wisconsin. After the 2020 census, the Wisconsin legislature, which is controlled by Republicans, drew new districting maps for both the state assembly and the state senate. Governor Tony Evers, a Democrat, vetoed these maps.

Lawsuits were brought in federal and state court challenging the existing districting. The Wisconsin Supreme Court asked the parties to submit new districting plans. The federal court lawsuit was put on hold. The Republican legislature submitted the same plan as before; it decreased the number of majority-Black districts in the assembly from six to five. Evers submitted a plan that increased the number of such districts to seven.

The Wisconsin Supreme Court then issued an order that prevented the use of the existing districts and that implemented the governor's plan. The state supreme court added, "there are good reasons to believe a seventh majority-Black district is needed to satisfy" the Voting Rights Act.[15]

On March 23, in *Wisconsin State Legislature v. Wisconsin Elections Commission*, the Supreme Court reversed the Wisconsin Supreme Court's decision adopting the governor's map and sent the case back to the state court. The Court said that in order for the Wisconsin Supreme Court to draw districts to create an additional majority Black district it needed to determine this was required by the Voting Rights Act.[16] The Court said no such finding had been made by the state court; it found only that "there are good reasons" to think that there was a violation of the Act. That is different from the required conclusion for relief: that the Act actually was violated.

Justice Sotomayor dissented, joined by Justice Kagan. She objected to the Court deciding matters such as this on the shadow docket without briefing or argument. She said that the Supreme Court's intervention "is not only extraordinary but also unnecessary" because the state court left open the possibility that someone could still bring a challenge to the maps. She said, "I would allow that process to unfold."[17]

## Implications

The Supreme Court has limited the power of lower courts—federal and state—to act before elections. Although these rulings are on the "shadow docket," they will have important implications for future election litigation. As the November 2022 election approaches and as the November 2024 election looms, these cases will matter in terms of the power of the federal courts to act.

## Endnotes

1. *See,* e.g., William Baude, Foreword: The Supreme Court's Shadow Docket, 9 *N.Y.U. J. L. & Liberty* 1, 1 (2015); Stephen I. Vladeck, The Solicitor General and the Shadow Docket, 133 *Harv. L. Rev.* 123, 123 (2019).

2. 142 S. Ct. 879 (2022).

3. Singleton v. Merrill, No. 2:21-CV-1291-AMM, 2022 WL 265001, at *2 (N.D. Ala. Jan. 24, 2022), *cert. granted sub nom.* Merrill v. Milligan 142 S. Ct. 879 (2022).

4. 142 S. Ct. 879, 884 (Kagan, J., dissenting).

5. *Id.* at 882 (Roberts, C.J., dissenting).

6. *Id.* at 879 (Kavanaugh, J., concurring).

7. Purcell v. Gonzalez, 549 U. S. 1, 3 (2006) (per curiam).

8. *Id.* at 5-6 (2006) (per curiam).

9. 140 S. Ct. 1205, 1206-07 (2020) (per curiam).

10. *Id.* at 1209 (Ginsburg, J., dissenting).

11. *Id.* at 1207 (Kavanaugh, J., concurring).

12. *Id.*

13. Ardoin v. Robinson, No. 21-1596, 2022 WL 2312680 (U.S. June 28, 2022).

14. Robinson v. Ardoin, No. CV 22-211-SDD-SDJ, 2022 WL 2012389, at *1 (M.D. La. June 6, 2022), *cert. granted before judgement,* No. 21-1596, 2022 WL 2312680 (U.S. June 28, 2022).

15. Johnson v. Wisconsin Elections Comm'n, 2022 WI 14, 400 Wis. 2d 626, 971 N.W.2d 402, 407 *cert. granted, opinion rev'd sub nom.* Wisconsin Legislature v. Wisconsin Elections Comm'n, 142 S. Ct. 1245 (2022).

16. 142 S. Ct. 1245, 1248 (2022) (Sotomayor, J., dissenting).

17. *Id.* at 1253.

# 7

# Federal Jurisdiction

The Supreme Court has said that the Eleventh Amendment bars suits against state governments in federal court. Under clearly established law, it does not matter whether the plaintiff is from that state or another state, or whether the relief sought is money damages or an injunction. State governments generally cannot be sued.

But there are some ways around this and some exceptions. For example, since *Ex parte Young*, in 1908, the Supreme Court has held that state officers may be sued for injunctive relief even when the state government itself cannot be named as a defendant.[1] This is a crucial way of holding state governments accountable.

Also, the Court has said that in limited circumstances, Congress, by statute, can abrogate sovereign immunity and authorize suits against state governments. Most importantly, the Court has ruled that Congress, when acting pursuant to its power under §5 of the Fourteenth Amendment, which empowers legislation to enforce the requirements of that amendment, may authorize suits against state government.[2]

The Court decided two matters concerning federal jurisdiction in October Term 2021. One, *Whole Woman's Health v. Jackson*, arose in the abortion context, but involves the question of whether state officers can be sued if they play no role in enforcing the state statute.[3] The other, *Torres v. Texas Department of Public Safety*, involves when Congress can authorize suits against state governments.[4]

## *Whole Woman's Health v. Jackson*

Texas adopted a law, S.B. 8, that prohibits abortion once the fetal heartbeat can be detected, which is about six weeks after a woman's last menstrual period. It thus prohibits abortions significantly before viability, which is about the twenty-fourth week of pregnancy, and before many women even know that they are pregnant. At the time Texas enacted this law, before the Court overruled *Roe v. Wade*, it was clearly unconstitutional.

The Texas law is not enforced by state or local government officials, but instead authorizes civil suits against doctors who perform abortions or against those who aid or abet abortions. Such individuals can be sued for $10,000. Thus S.B. 8 is enforced by private civil suits, not by government action. The law went into effect on September 1st and on that day, the Supreme Court, 5–4, refused a request to issue a preliminary injunction against it. A short *per curiam* opinion said that there was an unusual procedural dimension to the law in that it was enforced by private civil suits and not by government officials.[5] Chief Justice Roberts and Justices Breyer, Sotomayor, and Kagan strongly dissented and would have enjoined the law.

After the Court refused to enjoin the Texas law, the U.S. government filed suit to strike down S. B. 8. A federal district court ruled that the U.S. government had standing and the legal authority to sue and issued a preliminary injunction. The U.S. Court of Appeals for the Fifth Circuit, 2–1, stayed the district court's order pending briefing and oral argument, thus allowing the Texas law to go back into effect.

On October 21, 2021, the Supreme Court granted review in both cases and scheduled oral arguments for November 1. *Whole Woman's Health v. Jackson* involved whether state officials can be sued to enjoin an unconstitutional state law if they play no role in enforcing it. *United States v. Texas* concerned whether the U.S. government may sue to challenge a state law which infringes constitutional rights.[6]

It is important to recognize that both of these cases involved the issue of who may sue to challenge a state law that violates the Constitution;

neither posed the question of whether the Texas law was unconstitutional. In *Whole Woman's Health*, the Court limited the ability to sue state officers if they do not play a role in enforcing the law. The Court dismissed *United States v. Texas* as certiorari having been improvidently granted and thus did not issue a decision.

The Court, in *Whole Woman's Health*, in a 5–4 decision, ruled that state officers may be sued for injunctive relief only if they have a role in enforcing the law.[7] The Court also held, 8–1, that licensing officials in Texas play a role in enforcing S. B. 8 and thus could be sued to enjoin it.

Justice Gorsuch wrote the opinion for the Court and focused on what suits are permissible against state officials. He said that Texas state judges and court clerks could not be sued to enjoin S. B. 8:

> *But as* Ex parte Young *explained, this traditional exception does not normally permit federal courts to issue injunctions against state-court judges or clerks. Usually, those individuals do not enforce state laws as executive officials might; instead, they work to resolve disputes between parties. If a state court errs in its rulings, too, the traditional remedy has been some form of appeal, including to this Court, not the entry of an ex ante injunction preventing the state court from hearing cases.*[8]

The Court explained that the state court judges and clerks are not adverse parties and thus not appropriate as defendants in a suit seeking injunctive relief.

The Court next said that the Texas Attorney General could not be sued for an injunction because he plays no role in enforcing the law. While *Ex parte Young* authorizes federal courts to enjoin certain state officials from enforcing state laws, the Court emphasized that the attorney general of Texas does not have any enforcement in connection with S. B. 8 that a federal court might enjoin him from exercising. Justice Gorsuch wrote: "While *Ex parte Young* authorizes federal courts to enjoin certain state officials from enforcing state laws, the petitioners do not direct this Court to any enforcement authority the attorney general possesses in connection with S. B. 8 that a federal court might enjoin him from exercising."[9] Justice Gorsuch explained that an injunction is to restrain a person from acting; if state officials play no role in enforcing the law, then an injunction against them does not make sense.

The effect of this decision precludes suits against state officials for injunctions to enjoin laws that authorize money damages for exercising a constitutional right. Justice Gorsuch addressed this and said that remedies still exist. A person sued under S. B. 8, or any law authorizing civil suits, can argue as a defense that it is unconstitutional. Also, the Court said that challenges seeking injunctive relief might be brought in state court.[10] Justice Gorsuch said, "This Court has never recognized an unqualified right to pre-enforcement review of constitutional claims in federal court."[11]

Eight justices, all but Justice Thomas, agreed that the state licensing officials could be sued for injunctive relief because they play a role in enforcing the law. Justice Thomas said

> *even when there is an appropriate defendant to sue, a plaintiff may bring an action under* Ex parte Young *only when the defendant "threaten[s] and [is] about to commence proceedings." Our later cases explain that "the prospect of state suit must be imminent." Here, none of the licensing officials has threatened enforcement proceedings against petitioners because none has authority to bring them. Petitioners do not and cannot dispute this point.*[12]

That issue was remanded to the Fifth Circuit, which then certified the question to the Texas State Supreme Court to decide whether medical licensing boards play a role in enforcing S. B. 8. Of course, the importance of this issue changed dramatically after June 24, when the Court overruled *Roe v. Wade*. This means the Texas law prohibiting abortions after the sixth week of pregnancy is constitutional.

Chief Justice Roberts dissented and stressed the importance of an injunction against an unconstitutional law. He wrote:

> *These provisions, among others, effectively chill the provision of abortions in Texas. Texas says that the law also blocks any pre-enforcement judicial review in federal court. On that*

> *latter contention, Texas is wrong. As eight Members of the Court agree, petitioners may bring a pre-enforcement suit challenging the Texas law in federal court under* Ex parte Young, *because there exist state executive officials who retain authority to enforce it. Given the ongoing chilling effect of the state law, the District Court should resolve this litigation and enter appropriate relief without delay.*[13]

Roberts would have allowed the Attorney General to be sued, because "the Attorney General maintains authority coextensive with the Texas Medical Board to address violations of S. B. 8. The Attorney General may 'institute an action for a civil penalty' if a physician violates a rule or order of the Board."[14] He also would have allowed the court clerk to be sued for injunctive relief.

Most importantly, Roberts emphasized the importance of federal courts being available to hear challenges to the constitutionality of laws. He forcefully concluded his dissent:

> *The clear purpose and actual effect of S. B. 8 has been to nullify this Court's rulings. It is, however, a basic principle that the Constitution is the "fundamental and paramount law of the nation," and "[i]t is emphatically the province and duty of the judicial department to say what the law is." Marbury v. Madison (1803). Indeed, "[i]f the legislatures of the several states may, at will, annul the judgments of the courts of the United States, and destroy the rights acquired under those judgments, the constitution itself becomes a solemn mockery." The nature of the federal right infringed does not matter; it is the role of the Supreme Court in our constitutional system that is at stake.*[15]

Justice Sotomayor in dissent said, "The Court should have put an end to this madness months ago, before S. B. 8 first went into effect."[16] Justice Sotomayor said that *Ex parte Young* allows suits against state officers to enjoin unconstitutional laws and can be applied to permit a suit for an injunction in these circumstances. She expressed grave concerns about the implications of the Court's holding for the future. She wrote:

> *The dispute is over whether States may nullify federal constitutional rights by employing schemes like the one at hand. The Court indicates that they can, so long as they write their laws to more thoroughly disclaim all enforcement by state officials, including licensing officials. This choice to shrink from Texas' challenge to federal supremacy will have far-reaching repercussions. I doubt the Court, let alone the country, is prepared for them. . . . This is a brazen challenge to our federal structure.*[17]

After the Court's decision, some other states, such as Oklahoma and Idaho, copied and adopted S. B. 8. But the implications for federal jurisdiction extend far beyond the abortion context. A state can create civil liability for any constitutionally protected behavior and so long as no state official plays any role in enforcing it, the law will remain on the books until someone violates it, is sued, and challenges it. For instance, a state could create civil liability for anyone who performs a same-sex wedding or owns a gun or criticizes the governor. The state conceivably could set civil liability at a million dollars, so that no one would risk being sued. California has recently adopted a law creating civil liability for those who sell or distribute firearms under certain circumstances including ones that might be protected by the Second Amendment. To be clear, a person who violates the law and is sued can argue as a defense that the law is unconstitutional. But state officers may be sued for injunctive relief only if they play a role in enforcing the law.

## *Torres v. Texas Department of Public Safety*

Congress generally may authorize suits against state governments only when it is acting pursuant to §5 of the Fourteenth Amendment. Congress may not override the Eleventh Amendment when acting under any other constitutional authority. The seminal case holding that Congress can make states liable to suit in federal court pursuant to its powers under the post-Civil War amendments was *Fitzpatrick v. Bitzer* in 1976.[18] *Fitzpatrick* involved a suit brought directly against a state government pursuant to Title VII of the Civil Rights Act of 1964, which prohibits employment discrimination. Congress applied Title VII to the states under its powers under §5 of the Fourteenth Amendment. The Court reasoned that the Fourteenth Amendment specifically was intended to limit state sovereignty, and therefore congressional legislation under the Fourteenth Amendment can authorize suits directly against the states in federal court.

In 1996, in *Seminole Tribe of Florida v. Florida,* the Supreme Court held that Congress may abrogate the Eleventh Amendment only when acting under its §5 powers and not under any other constitutional authority.[19] This overruled a series of cases decided in the late 1980s in which the Supreme Court held that Congress may authorize suits when acting pursuant to other constitutional powers as long as the federal law, in its text, clearly and expressly permits federal court jurisdiction over state governments. The Court has applied its holding in *Seminole Tribe* to say that states cannot be sued pursuant to federal statutes for patent infringement,[20] copyright infringement,[21] employment discrimination in violation of the Age Discrimination in Employment Act,[22] or employment discrimination in violation of Title I of the Americans with Disabilities Act.[23]

The only exception to this has been for bankruptcy proceedings. In *Central Virginia Community College v. Katz*, the Supreme Court held that the Eleventh Amendment and sovereign immunity do not apply in bankruptcy proceedings at all.[24] Justice Stevens wrote for the Court in a 5–4 decision. He concluded that the clause in Article I, § 8 of the Constitution, empowering Congress to create uniform rules for bankruptcy, was meant to override considerations of sovereign immunity. The Court declared that the clause, its history, and the initial bankruptcy legislation enacted by Congress all "demonstrate that [the Bankruptcy Clause] was intended not just as a grant of legislative authority to Congress, but also to authorize limited subordination of state sovereign immunity in the bankruptcy arena."[25] The Court concluded that sovereign immunity does not apply at all in proceedings properly arising under the bankruptcy powers of Congress.

In *Torres v. Texas Department of Public Safety*, the Court recognized another area where Congress may authorize suits against state governments: Congress' power to raise an army and a navy.[26] The Uniformed Services Employment and Reemployment Rights Act of 1994 gives returning veterans the right to reclaim their prior jobs with state employers and requires that state governments use "reasonable efforts" to accommodate any service-related disability, or find an "equivalent" position (or its "nearest approximation") where such disability prevents the veteran from holding their prior position.[27] The statute authorizes suit if those employers refuse to accommodate them.

Le Roy Torres enlisted in the Army Reserves in 1989. In 2007, he was called to active duty and deployed to Iraq. While serving, Torres was exposed to toxic burn pits, a method of garbage disposal that sets open fire to all manner of trash, human waste, and military equipment.

Torres received an honorable discharge. He returned home with constrictive bronchitis, a respiratory condition that narrowed his airways and made breathing difficult. These ailments, Torres alleges, changed his life and left him unable to work at his old job as a state trooper. Torres asked his former employer, the Texas Department of Public Safety, to accommodate his condition by reemploying him in a different role. Texas refused to do so.

Torres sued Texas, contending that the state had violated USERRA's mandate that state employers rehire returning servicemembers, using "reasonable efforts" to accommodate any service-related disability. Texas claimed that sovereign immunity protected it from suit and that Congress acted unconstitutionally in authorizing suits against states.

The issue was whether Congress could abrogate sovereign immunity in acting under its power to regulate armies and navies. The Court ruled that Congress could do so. It was a 5–4 decision, with Justice Breyer writing the majority opinion and joined by Chief Justice Roberts and Justices Sotomayor, Kagan, and Kavanaugh. Justice Breyer emphasized Congress' broad powers to provide for the military. He wrote: "The Constitution vests in Congress the power '[t]o raise and support Armies' and '[t]o provide and maintain a Navy. Pursuant to that authority, Congress enacted a federal law that gives returning veterans the right to reclaim their prior jobs with state employers and authorizes suit if those employers refuse to accommodate them. *See* Uniformed Services Employment and Reemployment Rights Act of 1994 (USERRA)."[28] Justice Breyer explained that this case asks whether states may invoke sovereign immunity as a legal defense to block such suits. He concluded: "In our view, they cannot. Upon entering the Union, the States implicitly agreed that their sovereignty would yield to federal policy to build and keep a national military. States thus gave up their immunity from congressionally authorized suits pursuant to the 'plan of the Convention,' as part of 'the structure of the original Constitution itself.'"[29]

The Court stressed that the "Constitution's text, its history, and this Court's precedents show that 'when the States entered the federal system, they renounced their right' to interfere with national policy in this area."[30]

Justice Thomas wrote for the dissenting justices and strongly disagreed that Congress had the power to authorize suits against the states. He said that "constitutional text, history, and precedent all show that when the States ratified the Constitution, they did not implicitly consent to private damages actions filed in their own courts—whether authorized by Congress' war powers or any other Article I power."[31]

## Conclusion

Of the two cases, *Whole Woman's Health v. Jackson* is likely the more significant because it limits the ability to sue state officers in all contexts, while *Torres v. Texas Department of Public Safety* is a narrower ruling about the authority to sue states under one federal statute. Also, the former case is a major change in the law, while the latter adds one more instance where state governments can be sued. But both are important in clarifying crucial aspects of federal court jurisdiction and specifically the ability to hold state governments accountable in federal court litigation.

## Endnotes

1. 209 U.S. 123 (1908).
2. *See* Fitzpatrick v. Bitzer, 427 U.S. 445 (1976); Seminole Tribe of Fla. v. Fla., 517 U.S. 44 (1996).
3. 142 S. Ct. 522 (2021).
4. 142 S. Ct. 2455 (2022).
5. 142 S. Ct. 522 (2021) (per curiam).
6. United States v. Texas, 142 S. Ct. 522 (2021).
7. 142 S. Ct. at 534.

8. *Id.* at 532.
9. *Id.* at 534.
10. *Id.* at 537-38.
11. *Id.*
12. *Id.* at 542 (Thomas, J., dissenting) (internal citations omitted).
13. *Id.* at 544 (Roberts, C.J., dissenting) (internal citations omitted).
14. *Id.*
15. *Id.* at 545 (internal citation omitted).
16. *Id.* (Sotomayor, J., dissenting).
17. *Id.* at 550.
18. 427 U.S. 445 (1976).
19. 517 U.S. 44 (1996).
20. Fla. Prepaid Postsecondary Educ. Expense Bd. v. Coll. Sav. Bank, 527 U.S. 627 (1999).
21. Allen v. Cooper, 140 S. Ct. 994 (2020).
22. Kimel v. Fla. Bd. of Regents, 525 U.S. 1121 (1999).
23. Cedar Rapids Cmty. Sch. Dist. v. Garret F. ex rel. Charlene F., 526 U.S. 66 (1999).
24. 46 U.S. 356 (2006).
25. 546 U.S. at 363.
26. 142 S. Ct. 2455 (2022).
27. 38 U.S.C. § 4313(a)(3).
28. 142 S. Ct. at 2460 (internal citations omitted).
29. *Id.* (internal citations omitted). .
30. *Id.* at 2463 (internal citations omitted)..
31. *Id.* at 2470 (Thomas, J., dissenting).

8

# First Amendment: Freedom of Speech

In a term of dramatic rulings that significantly changed the law, the rulings about freedom of speech under the First Amendment were neither particularly ideological nor huge in their significance. But they did clarify some important aspects of free speech law: the distinction between content-based and content-neutral regulations, the government speech doctrine, and the issue of when a government action is an infringement of speech.

## Content-Based v. Content-Neutral Regulations

For decades, a central inquiry in free speech analysis has been whether the government regulation is content-based or content-neutral. Content-based government regulations of speech generally must meet strict scrutiny.[1] To be constitutional, they must be narrowly tailored to achieve a compelling government purpose. By contrast, content-neutral regulations only must meet intermediate scrutiny, being substantially related to achieve an important government purpose.[2]

Therefore, a great deal of First Amendment litigation focuses on whether a particular law or regulation should be deemed content-based or content-neutral. The Supreme Court's decision in *City of Austin v. Reagan National Advertising*, provides important guidance on how it is to be determined whether a law is content based.[3]

The case involved an Austin, Texas, ordinance regulating digital signs on buildings. The city allowed digital signs for businesses operating on the premises of a building, but generally prohibited signs for off-premises activities. The city's sign code defined the term "off-premise sign" as "a sign advertising a business, person, activity, goods, products, or services not located on the site where the sign is installed, or that directs persons to any location not on that site." The code prohibited the construction of any new off-premises signs but allowed existing off-premises signs to remain as grandfathered "non-conforming signs." The city said that its goal is to "protect the aesthetic value of the city and to protect public safety."

The U.S. Court of Appeals for the Fifth Circuit found the Austin ordinance to be an unconstitutional restriction on speech. The Fifth Circuit explained that the city's on-/off-premises distinction required a reader to inquire "who is the speaker and what is the speaker saying," "both hallmarks of a content-based inquiry."[4] It reasoned that "[t]he fact that a government official ha[s] to read a sign's message to determine the sign's purpose [i]s enough to" render a regulation content based and "subject [it] to strict scrutiny."[5]

The Fifth Circuit justified its decision based on the Supreme Court's ruling in *Reed v. Town of Gilbert* (2015).[6] In that case, the Court struck down a municipal ordinance that regulated the presence of outdoor signs, but that had 23 categories of exceptions. For example, under the ordinance, political signs could be quite large and remain up throughout the election season, while signs giving directions to events had to be small and could be posted for only a short time. The Court unanimously declared this unconstitutional. The Court said that "[o]n its face, the Sign Code is a content-based regulation of speech."[7] The Fifth Circuit said that the Austin ordinance was likewise content-based: the sign was allowed if its message was about businesses on the premises, but it wasn't allowed if the sign was about off-premises businesses.

In a 6–3 decision, the Supreme Court reversed the Fifth Circuit and found that the Austin regulation of digital signs is content-neutral. The Court remanded the case for the application of intermediate scrutiny.

Justice Sotomayor wrote the opinion for the Court. The Court stressed that a government regulation is content based if it discriminates based on "the topic discussed or the idea or message expressed."[8] In other words, a law is content-based if the regulation of speech is based on the subject matter (the topic discussed) or the viewpoint (the ideology of the message). If the law applies to all speech, regardless of the subject matter and the viewpoint, then it is content-neutral and only need meet intermediate scrutiny. Justice Sotomayor added at the end of her opinion that "[i]f there is evidence that an impermissible purpose or justification underpins a facially content-neutral restriction, for instance, that restriction may be content based."[9]

The Court explicitly distinguished *Reed v. Town of Gilbert*. The Court explained that what was allowed under the ordinance in that case depended on the topic of the sign. Political messages were treated differently and more favorably than signs for gatherings for other activities, such as for religious worship.

The Court rejected the Fifth Circuit's conclusion that a regulation cannot be content neutral if it requires reading the sign at issue. Justice Sotomayor wrote, "Unlike the regulations at issue in Reed, the City's off-premises distinction requires an examination of speech only in service of drawing neutral, location-based lines. It is agnostic as to content."[10] The Court explained, "A sign's substantive message itself is irrelevant to the application of the provisions; there are no content-discriminatory classifications for political messages, ideological messages, or directional messages. . . . Rather, the City's provisions distinguish based on location: A given sign is treated differently based solely on whether it is located on the same premises as the thing being discussed or not."[11] The Court thought of the Austin regulation as being like a time, place, or manner restriction concerning speech.

The Court did not declare the Austin ordinance unconstitutional but remanded the case to determine whether it was permissible under intermediate scrutiny. It will be interesting to see on remand whether the on-premises/off-premises distinction is found to contribute to aesthetics or public safety. Is a sign for businesses on the premises more likely to be attractive or less likely to be distracting?

Justice Breyer wrote a concurring opinion in which he recognized *Reed v. Town of Gilbert* as binding precedent but said that "I write separately because I continue to believe that the Court's reasoning in *Reed* was wrong."[12] Justice Breyer criticized *Reed*'s use of strict scrutiny. He urged the Court to avoid the use of strict scrutiny and instead to use a "proportionality analysis," and says that he "would weigh the First Amendment harms that a regulation imposes against the regulatory objectives that it serves." He would uphold the City of Austin's regulation because it causes no "disproportionate harm."

Justice Alito concurred in the judgment in part and dissented in part. He said that the challengers failed to meet their burden for a facial attack on a statute: demonstrating "no set of circumstances exists under which the [law] would be valid, or show that the law lacks a plainly legitimate sweep."[13] Nor, according to Justice Alito, were the requirements for a successful overbreadth challenge met.

Justice Thomas, joined by Justices Gorsuch and Barrett dissented. They maintained that under *Reed*, the Austin ordinance was content-based. If the content of the ad was for a business on the premises, the ad was allowed; if the content as for some other business, it wasn't permitted. That, the dissent contended, was a content-based restriction that warranted strict scrutiny. The dissent said that the Court "misinterprets *Reed*'s clear rule for content-based restrictions and replaces it with an incoherent and malleable standard."[14]

The distinction between the majority and the dissent is subtle, but important. The dissent would find any regulation that depends on the looking at what is said in the message as requiring strict scrutiny. The Austin regulation does that because if the message advertises what is on the premises it is allowed, but an advertisement for anything else is not allowed.

But the majority defines content-based more narrowly. For the Court a law is content-based if it is a subject matter restriction, focused on the topic of the speech, or a viewpoint restriction, focused on the ideology of the message. If it is neither, it is content-neutral, and only intermediate scrutiny is used. In this way, perhaps the greatest significance of the case is in what the Court didn't do: it did not adopt the dissent's broad approach for finding that laws are content-based and must meet strict scrutiny.

*Town of Reed v. Gilbert* caused great confusion in the lower courts. *City of Austin v. Reagan National Advertising* provides important clarification and guidance.

## *Shurtleff v. City of Boston*

The Supreme Court has held that when the government is the speaker the First Amendment's free speech clause does not apply at all or provide a basis for challenging the government's action. For example, in *Pleasant Grove, Utah v. Summum*,[15] the Court held that a city that had monuments in its park could choose what to include and deny a request from a private group to have a monument to its faith placed there. The Court explained that the park and its display was government speech.

The Court returned to this issue in *Walker v. Texas Division, Sons of Confederate Veterans*, where in a 5–4 decision the Court held that the Texas Department of Motor Vehicles did not violate the First Amendment in refusing to issue a license plate with the confederate battle flag.[16]

Texas, like all states, requires license plates on cars. In Texas, people can have either the general type of plate issued by the state, or they may have specialty plates. For one type of specialty plate, a nonprofit organization asked the Texas Department of Motor Vehicles Board to approve a design and then issue plates with it. The Texas Division of the Sons of Confederate Veterans proposed a specialty license plate design featuring a confederate battle flag, but the board rejected the proposal.

The Supreme Court held that the board did not violate the First Amendment because license plates are government speech and when the government is the speaker it cannot violate the speech clause of the First Amendment. Justice Breyer, writing for the majority, said: "When government speaks, it is not barred by the Free Speech Clause from determining the content of what it says."[17] The Court explained: "Were the Free Speech Clause interpreted otherwise, government would not work." The government must be able to express messages such as to encourage recycling or energy conservation or vaccination of children. The Court said that the license plate is government speech and therefore the choice of the board to not allow the confederate flag does not violate the First Amendment.

Thus, the crucial distinction under the First Amendment is whether the government itself is the speaker, in which case the First Amendment does not apply, or whether the government is creating a forum for private speech and the government must comply with the First Amendment. *Shurtleff v. City of Boston* concerns this distinction.[18]

There are flag poles at Boston City Hall and since 2005, the city has allowed groups to hold flag-raising ceremonies on the plaza. Participants may hoist a flag of their choosing on the third flagpole (in place of the city's flag) and fly it for the duration of the event, typically a couple of hours. Between 2005 and 2017, there were 284 requests by private groups to raise flags and in 284 instances the city granted the request. Never had it refused a request.

In July 2017, Harold Shurtleff, the director of an organization called Camp Constitution, asked to raise a Christian flag as part of a ceremony to "commemorate the civic and social contributions of the Christian community." The flag was a red cross on a blue field against a white background.

The commissioner of Boston's Property Management Department rejected the request. The commissioner worried that flying a religious flag at City Hall could violate the Constitution's Establishment Clause and found no record of Boston ever having raised such a flag.

Shurtleff sued. Both the federal district court and the U.S. Court of Appeals for the First Circuit ruled against him, concluding that the flagpole was a place of government speech. The Supreme Court unanimously reversed. Justice Breyer wrote the opinion for the Court and said that the crucial question was whether the flag should be regarded as government speech. He noted that "the boundary between government speech and private expression can blur when, as here, a government invites the people to participate in a program. In those situations, when does government-public engagement transmit the government's own message? And when does it instead create a forum for the expression of private speakers' views?"[19]

Justice Breyer said that, "In answering these questions, we conduct a holistic inquiry designed to determine whether the government intends to speak for itself or to regulate private expression. . . . Our past cases have looked to several types of evidence to guide the analysis, including: the history of the expression at issue; the public's likely perception as to who (the government or a private person) is speaking; and the extent to which the government has actively shaped or controlled the expression."[20]

Applying these factors, the Court concluded that Boston had created a forum for private speech. Decisive to the Court's analysis was that Boston had allowed private flags to be raised in every other instance where there was a request. The Court concluded that allowing a private group to raise its flag with a cross did not violate the Establishment Clause of the First Amendment. In fact, he explained, "When a government does not speak for itself, it may not exclude speech based on 'religious viewpoint'; doing so 'constitutes impermissible viewpoint discrimination.'"[21]

The decision reaffirms the distinction between the government as speaker as opposed to the government creating a forum for private speech. Although the Court saw this as an easy case, Justice Breyer's opinion will be significant in the future in articulating some criteria to use in drawing this distinction. To the extent that the Court brushed aside concerns about the Establishment Clause, that was in accord with the decisions this term that were directly about the religion clauses that are discussed in the next chapter.

## *Houston Community College System v. Wilson*

A crucial question in free speech litigation—like that for every constitutional right—is whether the government action constitutes an infringement of the right. Only if there is an infringement does the First Amendment apply and the government must meet the requisite level of scrutiny.

*Houston Community College System v. Wilson* ultimately is about the question of whether there was an infringement of speech.[22] David Wilson is an elected member of the Houston Community College Board of Trustees, which oversees community colleges. There are nine members of the Board, and each is elected to a six-year term.

Wilson was in frequent disagreement with the other members of the Board, including bringing several lawsuits against them. At a 2018 meeting, the Board passed a resolution "censuring" Wilson. The resolution stated that Mr. Wilson's conduct was "not consistent with the best interests of the College" and "not only inappropriate, but reprehensible." The resolution provided that Wilson was "ineligible for election to Board officer positions for the 2018 calendar year," that he was "ineligible for reimbursement for any College-related travel, . . ." and that his future requests to "access . . . funds in his Board account for community affairs" would require Board approval.[23]

Wilson sued the Board and the other members, claiming that the censure resolution violated his free speech rights. The Supreme Court, in an opinion by Justice Neil Gorsuch, unanimously ruled against Wilson. In part, the Court relied on a long history of elected bodies—including the U.S. Senate and House of Representatives—censuring members for perceived misconduct. The Court explained, "If anything, censures along these lines have proven more common yet at the state and local level. If this longstanding practice does not "put at rest" the question of the Constitution's meaning for the dispute before us, it surely leaves a "considerable impression."[24]

The Court went further and said that the censure resolution should not be seen as an "adverse action" that is an infringement of speech. Justice Gorsuch explained that those who run for public office expose themselves to criticism for their performance. Moreover, the Court stressed that the censure resolution was itself speech by the other members of the Board. It explained:

> *The censure at issue before us was a form of speech by elected representatives. It concerned the public conduct of another elected representative. Everyone involved was an equal member of the same deliberative body. As it comes to us, too, the censure did not prevent Mr. Wilson from doing his job, it did not deny him any privilege of office, and Mr. Wilson does not allege it was defamatory. At least in these circumstances, we do not see how the Board's censure could have materially deterred an elected official like Mr. Wilson from exercising his own right to speak.*[25]

The Court left open the possibility that there may be other instances in which censure resolutions have enough consequences, and significant chilling effect, to violate the First Amendment. But this was not such a case. Notably, the Court came to this conclusion by finding no tangible adverse effects on Wilson, notwithstanding his claim that the censure resolution would have adverse financial consequences for him.

## Endnotes

1. *See, e.g.,* R.A.V. v. City of St. Paul, 505 U.S. 377, 382 (1992); United States v. Alvarez, 567 U.S. 709, 717 (2012) (plurality opinion).
2. *See, e.g.,* Turner Broad. Sys. v. Fed. Commc'n Comm'n, 512 U.S. 622, 642 (1994).
3. *See* City of Austin v. Reagan Nat'l Advert. of Austin, LLC.,142 S.Ct. 1464 (2022).
4. Reagan Nat. Advert. of Austin, Inc. v. City of Austin, 972 F.3d 696, 706 (5th Cir. 2020); *see also* Reed v. Town of Gilbert, 576 U.S. 155 (2015).
5. *Id.*
6. 576 U.S. at 155 (2015).
7. *Id.* at 164.
8. 142 S. Ct. at 1474 (plurality opinion).
9. *Id.* at 1475.
10. *Id.* at 1471.
11. *Id.* at 1472.
12. *Id.* at 1476 (Breyer, J., concurring).
13. *Id.* at 1479 (Alito, concurring in the judgment).
14. *Id.* at 1481 (Thomas, J., dissenting).
15. *See* Pleasant Grove v. Summum, 555 U.S. 460 (2009).
16. Walker v. Texas Div., Sons of Confed. Veterans, 576 U.S. 200 (plurality opinion).
17. *Id.* at 200.
18. 142 S. Ct. at 1583 (2022).
19. *Id.* at 1589 (plurality opinion).
20. *Id.* at 1590. *See also* Walker, 576 U.S. 200.
21. *Id.* (quoting Good News Club v. Milford Central School, 533 U.S. 98, 112 (2001).
22. 142 S. Ct. at 1253 (2022).
23. *Id.* at 1258.
24. *Id.* at 1260 (quoting M'Culloch v. State, 17 U.S. 316, 410).
25. *Id.* at 1261.

# 9

# First Amendment: Religion

There is a deep political divide on the Supreme Court, and in the country, over the Constitution and religion. Liberals long have interpreted the Establishment Clause of the First Amendment as best understood through Thomas Jefferson's metaphor that there should be a wall separating church and state.[1] For decades, this was the approach taken by the Supreme Court, but conservatives reject this notion and believe that the government violates the Establishment Clause only if it coerces religious participation or gives assistance that favors some religions over others.

Conservatives favor strong protection of free exercise of religion, including to provide exemptions from laws prohibiting discrimination. Liberals, by contrast, favor the Court's adherence to its decision in *Employment Division v. Smith*—an opinion written by Justice Antonin Scalia—which held that the free exercise clause is not a basis for exemptions to laws of general applicability that were not motivated by a desire to infringe religion.[2]

The Court decided three cases about religion in October Term 2021. One, *Ramirez v. Collier*,[3] was statutory, interpreting the Religious Land Use and Institutional Persons Act. The other two—*Carson v. Makin*[4] and

*Kennedy v. Bremerton School District*[5]—involved the First Amendment. All three strongly protected free exercise of religion; never did the Court's majority express concerns over the Establishment Clause. That was left to the dissenting opinions.

## *Ramirez v. Collier*

John Ramirez was convicted of murder and sentenced to death in Texas, which carries out executions by lethal injection. He wanted his pastor, who was to be with him in the death chamber, to be able to touch him at the time of the execution and pray out loud. Texas forbids both the laying of hands and audible prayer in the death chamber.

The Court ruled 8–1 in favor of Ramirez. Chief Justice John Roberts wrote the opinion for the Court and only Justice Clarence Thomas dissented. The Court based its decision on the Religious Land Use and Institutionalized Persons Act, which says, in part, that the government must meet strict scrutiny if it significantly burdens the religious freedom of institutionalized individuals.

The Court said that the government failed to show that prohibiting touching or vocal prayer was necessary to achieve its goal of carrying out executions without disruption or obstruction. The Court pointed to a long history of allowing prayers by clergy at the time of executions and found that prohibiting touching was not the least restrictive way of meeting the state's interests. The Court thus concluded that Ramirez was likely to prevail on the merits of his claims that restrictions on religious touch and audible prayer in the execution chamber would impermissibly burden his religious freedom.

Most importantly, the Court applied a very rigorous strict scrutiny test, stressing the need for the government to show its action is necessary—the least restrictive way—to achieve its goal. The decision indicates that for cases under this statute, and likewise for the Religious Freedom Restoration Act, the Court will strongly protect free exercise of religion. The government must demonstrate a compelling interest and must meet the burden of showing that there is no other way to achieve its objective.

## *Carson v. Makin*

There are parts of Maine that are too rural to support public school systems. In these areas, school administrative units provide money for parents to send their children to private school. State law requires that the funds be used for secular schools; they cannot be used for "sectarian" education. Maine says that its goal is to provide a free secular education for every child in the state. Also, it does not want to use tax dollars to support religion. About 5,000 children are affected.

Two families brought a challenge arguing that prohibiting the use of funds in religious schools violates free exercise of religion. The Supreme Court, in a 6–3 decision, held in their favor. Chief Justice Roberts wrote the majority opinion, while both Justices Breyer and Sotomayor wrote dissenting opinions. The Court broadly ruled that the government cannot constitutionally deny funding for religious education when it funds secular private education. The Court declared that "we have repeatedly held that a State violates the Free Exercise Clause when it excludes religious observers from otherwise available public benefits."[6]

Prior to 2017, just five years ago, the Court never in American history had held that free exercise of religion required the government to subsidize religion. That case, *Trinity Lutheran v. Comer*, concluded that Missouri violated free exercise of religion when it subsidized surfacing playgrounds for public schools and secular private schools, but not religious schools.[7] The Court said that such discrimination against religion must meet strict scrutiny and rejected Missouri's argument that its interest in avoiding establishment of religion justified its action. Chief Justice Roberts, who also wrote that majority opinion, included a footnote stressing that the case was just about money for surfacing playgrounds.[8]

Three years later, in *Espinoza v. Montana Department of Revenue*, the Court declared unconstitutional a Montana program that provided tax credits to donors who sponsored scholarships for private school tuition.[9] The Montana Supreme Court declared that the program in funding religious schools violated a provision of the Montana Constitution that barred government aid to any school controlled in whole or in part by a church, sect, or denomination. The Court, in a 5–4 decision with the majority opinion again written by Chief Justice Roberts, said that Montana violated the Free Exercise Clause. The Court said that the program violated the Constitution because it "bar[red] religious schools from public benefits solely because of the religious character of the schools."[10] Chief Justice Roberts wrote: "A State need not subsidize private education, . . . [b]ut once a State decides to do so, it cannot disqualify some private schools solely because they are religious."[11]

In *Carson v. Makin*, the Court said that these two precedents resolve this case and are clear that the Maine law is unconstitutional. Chief Justice Roberts explained, "The 'unremarkable' principles applied in *Trinity Lutheran* and *Espinoza* suffice to resolve this case. Maine offers its citizens a benefit: tuition assistance payments for any family whose school district does not provide a public secondary school. . . . By 'condition[ing] the availability of benefits' in that manner, Maine's tuition assistance program—like the program in *Trinity Lutheran*—'effectively penalizes the free exercise' of religion.'"[12] In other words, whenever the government provides aid to private secular schools it is constitutionally required to make that aid available to religious institutions as well.

Justice Breyer, in his dissent, lamented the Court's ignoring of the Establishment Clause. He said that a key goal of that provision was to force people from having to support religions that they do not practice. He wrote: "As Thomas Jefferson, one of the leading drafters and proponents of those Clauses, wrote, 'to compel a man to furnish contributions of money for the propagation of opinions which he disbelieves, is sinful and tyrannical."' And as James Madison, another drafter and proponent, said, compelled taxpayer sponsorship of religion 'is itself a signal of persecution,' which 'will destroy that moderation and harmony which the forbearance of our laws to intermeddle with Religion, has produced amongst its several sects.'"[13] Breyer chastised the Court for giving no weight to Maine's interest in following the words of Jefferson and Madison and not using tax dollars from some to support the religions of others. It means that if Maine does not want to financially support religious education, then it must deny funds for secular private education as well.

Justice Sotomayor wrote a separate dissent and also cricitized the Court's abandonmentof the Establishment Clause. She began her dissenting opinon. "This Court continues to dismantle the wall of separation between church and state that the Framers fought to build. . . . [T]his Court should not have started down this path five years ago. See *Trinity Lutheran Church of Columbia, Inc.* v. *Comer* (2017)."[14]

She powerfully concluded her dissenting opinion:

> *What a difference five years makes. In 2017, I feared that the Court was "lead[ing] us . . . to a place where separation of church and state is a constitutional slogan, not a constitutional commitment." Today, the Court leads us to a place where separation of church and state becomes a constitutional violation. If a State cannot offer subsidies to its citizens without being required to fund religious exercise, any State that values its historic antiestablishment interests more than this Court does will have to curtail the support it offers to its citizens. With growing concern for where this Court will lead us next, I respectfully dissent.*[15]

*Carson v. Makin*, along with *Trinity Lutheran* and *Espinoza*, mark a significant change in the law. For decades, the issue before the Court was determining when *may* the government provide assistance to religious schools without violating the Establishment Clause of the First Amendment. Now the Court says that the Free Exercise Clause means that the government *must* provide aid for religious schools whenever it subsidizes secular private education.

The Court's holding is sure to lead to more litigation. Throughout the country, including in California, public school systems pay for charter schools. The law has been that the charter schools must be secular. But now there will be challenges arguing that the refusal to pay for religious charter schools violates free exercise of religion.

These challenges likely will not be limited to the school context. If the government provides funds for historic preservation of buildings, then it will argued that it is required to subsidize this for maintaining churches, synagogues, and mosques. If the government pays for alcohol or drug rehabilitation programs, then it will be contended that it has to subsidize faith-based programs.

The decision in *Carson v. Makin* reflects the very strong disagreement between the majority and dissenting justices over the relative importance of the Free Exercise and Establishment Clauses. The liberal justices see the

Establishment Clause as restricting government aid to religious institutions, while the conservatives see the Free Exercise Clause as requiring it when the government is providing financial support to private secular institutions.

## *Kennedy v. Bremerton School District*

In the early 1960s, the Supreme Court held that prayer in public schools, even voluntary prayer, violates the Establishment Clause of the First Amendment.[16] The Court has strictly adhered to this for 60 years. In *Wallace v. Jaffree* (1985), the Court declared unconstitutional an Alabama law that required that every school begin each day with a moment of silent prayer.[17] In *Lee v. Weisman* (1992), the Court held that clergy-delivered prayers at public school graduations are unconstitutional.[18] In *Santa Fe Independent School District v. Doe* (2000), the Court ruled that student-led prayers at high school football games violate the First Amendment.[19]

*Kennedy v. Bremerton School District* is the first Supreme Court decision to find that a teacher's prayer in a public school setting was constitutionally permissible. Indeed, the Court held that restricting this violated the teacher's free speech and free exercise of religion rights.

One unusual aspect of the case was the substantial disagreement between the majority and the dissent as to the facts of the case.[20] In fact, the dissent included a photograph to support its version of what had happened. Joseph Kennedy was the football coach at a public school in Bremerton, Washington. After games, Kennedy, a devout Christian, would kneel at the 50-yard line and engage in a prayer for about 30 seconds. This necessarily meant that spectators—students, parents, and community members—would observe Kennedy's religious conduct. Several games into his first season as coach, players began to join him and this grew to include a majority of the team. Sometimes opposing players were invited to join as well. A parent complained to the principal that his son "felt compelled to participate" in Kennedy's religious activity, even though he was an atheist, because "he felt he wouldn't get to play as much if he didn't participate."[21]

Over time, Kennedy began giving short motivational speeches at midfield after the games. Students, coaches, and other attendees from both teams were invited to participate. During the speeches, the participants kneeled around Kennedy. He then raised a helmet from each team and delivered a message containing religious content including prayers. The school district ordered that Kennedy cease his religious activities. He initially complied and then openly defied the order and was suspended.

Kennedy sued and argued that the school district had violated his First Amendment rights to freedom of speech and free exercise of religion. The federal district court and the Ninth Circuit ruled against him, stressing the school district's interest in complying with the ban on prayer in public schools. But the Supreme Court, in a 6-3 decision, ruled in his favor on both the speech and religion claims. The majority opinion characterized this case about a football coach who after the game wanted to engage in a moment of silent, private prayer. The dissent saw this as a football coach who was engaging in public prayers, sometimes joined by players and others, in the midst of a crowded football stadium. The dissenting opinions included pictures to show that the event was not private at all; the photographs showed the coach surrounded by players.

Justice Neil Gorsuch wrote the majority opinion. His opening paragraph reveals how the majority saw the facts and the law in this case:

> *Joseph Kennedy lost his job as a high school football coach because he knelt at midfield after games to offer a quiet prayer of thanks. Mr. Kennedy prayed during a period when school employees were free to speak with a friend, call for a reservation at a restaurant, check email, or attend to other personal matters. He offered his prayers quietly while his students were otherwise occupied. Still, the Bremerton School District disciplined him anyway.*[22]

The Court said:

> *Both the Free Exercise and Free Speech Clauses of the First Amendment protect expressions like Mr. Kennedy's. Nor does a proper understanding of the Amendment's Establishment Clause require the government to single out private religious speech for special disfavor. The Constitution and the best of our*

> *traditions counsel mutual respect and tolerance, not censorship and suppression, for religious and nonreligious views alike.*[23]

The Court explained that the School District's action against Kennedy violated his free exercise of religion because they "were neither neutral nor generally applicable. By its own admission, the District sought to restrict Mr. Kennedy's actions at least in part because of their religious character."[24]

The Court also said that the District violated Kennedy's free speech rights. Under *Garcetti v. Ceballos*,[25] there is no First Amendment protection for the speech of government employees on the job in the scope of their duties. But the Court concluded that Kennedy's speech was private speech and not government speech and thus had First Amendment protection. Justice Gorsuch wrote:

> *Applying these lessons here, it seems clear to us that Mr. Kennedy has demonstrated that his speech was private speech, not government speech. When Mr. Kennedy uttered the three prayers that resulted in his suspension, he was not engaged in speech "ordinarily within the scope" of his duties as a coach. He did not speak pursuant to government policy. He was not seeking to convey a government-created message. He was not instructing players, discussing strategy, encouraging better on-field performance, or engaged in any other speech the District paid him to produce as a coach. Simply put: Mr. Kennedy's prayers did not "ow[e their] existence" to Mr. Kennedy's responsibilities as a public employee."*[26]

The Court rejected the conclusion of the lower courts that allowing Kennedy's prayer would violate the Establishment Clause. The Court said that the lower courts relied on *Lemon v. Kurtzman*, which held that the government violates the Establishment Clause if it acts with the purpose of advancing religion, or if the primary effect is to advance or inhibit religion, or if there is excessive government entanglement with religion.[27] The Court had said that under this test, the government violates the Establishment Clause if the reasonable observer would perceive a government endorsement of religion.[28]

But Justice Gorsuch writing for the majority said "this Court long ago abandoned *Lemon* and its endorsement test offshoot."[29] The Court then said: "In place of *Lemon* and the endorsement test, this Court has instructed that the Establishment Clause must be interpreted by 'reference to historical practices and understandings.' '[T]he line' that courts and governments 'must draw between the permissible and the impermissible' has to 'accor[d] with history and faithfully reflec[t] the understanding of the Founding Fathers.'"[30]

The Court said that government coercion violates the Establishment Clause, but found insufficient evidence of that in this case. The Court did not articulate a test for determining what is impermissible coercion.

Justice Alito wrote a brief concurring opinion. He stressed that what makes this permissible is that the coach engaged in the prayer in a "lull" during the official activities: "The expression at issue in this case is unlike that in any of our prior cases involving the free-speech rights of public employees. Petitioner's expression occurred while at work but during a time when a brief lull in his duties apparently gave him a few free moments to engage in private activities. When he engaged in this expression, he acted in a purely private capacity."[31] Apart from the religion context, government employees are likely to focus on this and see it as expanding their free speech rights while on the job so long as the expression occurs in a "lull" in official duties.

Justice Sotomayor wrote a dissent, joined by Justices Breyer and Kagan, strongly disagreeing with the majority. She said that the majority, like in *Carson v. Makin,* "yet again [was] paying almost exclusive attention to the Free Exercise Clause's protection for individual religious exercise while giving short shrift to the Establishment Clause's prohibition on state establishment of religion."[32]

The dissent objected to the overruling of the *Lemon* test and to allowing prayer in public schools. Justice Sotomayor wrote:

> *The Court overrules* Lemon v. Kurtzman *(1971), and calls into question decades of subsequent precedents that it deems "offshoot[s]" of that decision. In the process, the Court rejects longstanding concerns surrounding government endorsement of religion and replaces the standard for reviewing such ques-*

> *tions with a new 'history and tradition' test. In addition, while the Court reaffirms that the Establishment Clause prohibits the government from coercing participation in religious exercise, it applies a nearly toothless version of the coercion analysis, failing to acknowledge the unique pressures faced by students when participating in school-sponsored activities. This decision does a disservice to schools and the young citizens they serve, as well as to our Nation's longstanding commitment to the separation of church and state.*[33]

What will this mean for prayer in public schools? It would seem that a teacher can pray before school, during recess, during lunch, after school, or any time during what Justice Alito calls "lulls" in school activities. This does not violate the Establishment Clause, even if students join in the prayers. But where the line will be drawn is sure to be much litigated. The Court's exclusive focus is on "history" and "the understanding of the Founding Fathers." But it is hard to ask what the Founding Fathers thought about prayer at high school football games or even about prayer in public schools because they did not exist in 1791 when the First Amendment was adopted. At the very least, the Court has opened the door to prayer in public schools more than it has been since the early 1960s. More generally, what will this mean for the many cases decided over a half century under the *Lemon* test.

## Conclusion

For decades, the Supreme Court took a robust approach to the Establishment Clause and provided relatively weak protections under the Free Exercise Clause. Now, though, the Court is taking the exactly the opposite course, finding little that violates the Establishment Clause and creating robust protections under the Free Exercise Clause. The implications of this shift are enormous.

## Endnotes

1. Thomas Jefferson, Draft Reply to the Danbury Baptist Association, *in* 36 The Papers of Thomas Jefferson, 1 December 1801 to 3 March 1802, 254-56 (Barbara B. Oberg. eds., 2009). I discuss the competing perspectives of the religion clauses in Howard Gillman & Erwin Chemerinsky, The Religion Clauses: The Case for Separating Church and State (2020).
2. Emp. Div., Dep't of Hum. Res. of Oregon v. Smith, 494 U.S. 872 (1990).
3. 142 S. Ct. 1264 (2022).
4. 142 S. Ct. 1987 (2022).
5. 142 S. Ct. 2407 (2022).
6. 142 S. Ct. at 1996.
7. Trinity Lutheran Church of Columbia, Inc. v. Comer, 137 S. Ct. 2012.
8. *Id.* at 2024 n. 3.
9. 140 S. Ct. 2246.
10. *Id.* at 2254.
11. *Id.* at 2261..
12. *Id.* at 1997 (internal citations omitted).
13. *Id.* at 2005 (Breyer, J., dissenting) (internal citations omitted).
14. *Id.* at 2012 (Sotomayor, J. dissenting).
15. *Id.* at 2014-15 (internal citations omitted).
16. Engel v. Vitale, 370 U.S. 421 (1962); Sch. Dist. of Abington Twp., Pa. v. Schempp, 374 U.S. 203 (1963).
17. 472 U.S. 38.
18. 505 U.S. 577.
19. 530 U.S. 290.
20. *See,* e.g, 142 S. Ct. at 2436 (Sotomayor, J., dissenting)(making the rare decision of actually including a picture of photograph of "J. Kennedy standing in a group of kneeling players" in her dissent).
21. Kennedy v. Bremerton Sch. Dist., 991 F.3d 1004, 1011 (9th Cir. 2021).
22. 142 S. Ct. at 2415.
23. 142 S. Ct. at 2415-2416.
24. *Id.* at 2422.
25. 547 U.S. 410 (2006).
26. 142 S. Ct. at 2424 (internal citations omitted).
27. 403 U.S. 602, 612-613.
28. *See, e.g., Capitol Square Rev. & Advisory Bd. v. Pinette*, 515 U.S. 753, 777 (O'Connor, J., concurring) ( stating "when the reasonable observer would view a government practice as endorsing religion, I believe that it is our duty to hold the practice invalid.")

29. 142 S. Ct. at 2427.
30. *Id.* at 2428 (internal citations omitted) (internal quotation marks omitted).
31. 142 S. Ct. at 2433-34 (Alito, J., concurring).
32. *Id.* at 2434 (Sotomayor, J., dissenting).
33. *Id.* (internal citations omitted).

# 10

# Immigration Law

Again, this term, the Court decided several cases on issues of immigration law. The highest profile of the cases, *Biden v. Texas*, upheld the authority of the Biden administration to repeal the Trump administration's controversial "remain in Mexico" program, which required those seeking asylum in the United States to stay in Mexico while their petitions were being considered.[1] But the other three cases all ruled against the claims of migrants who were seeking more protections under federal immigration law. These cases limited the ability of federal courts to provide relief to those challenging immigration procedures.

## *Biden v. Texas*

In 2018, the Trump administration adopted the Migrant Protection Protocol, which provided that those from other countries coming through Mexico and seeking asylum in the United States were required to remain in Mexico. This was a very controversial policy, and a legal challenge was pending in the Courts. The Biden administration rescinded the policy, but Texas and Missouri brought challenges to this.

The Supreme Court, in a 5–4 decision, ruled in favor of the Biden administration. Chief Justice Roberts wrote the majority opinion, which was joined by Justices Breyer, Sotomayor, Kagan, and Kavanaugh. The Court focused on the language of Section 1225(b)(2)(C) of the Immigration and Nationality Act, which provides that the federal government "may" return an asylum seeker who arrives at the U.S. border with Mexico or Canada to that country to await a hearing.

The Court explained that the use of the word "may," provides that the government has the discretion to return asylum seekers, but it is not required to do so. Chief Justice Roberts wrote:

> *The statute says "may." And "may" does not just suggest discretion, it "clearly connotes" it. Congress's use of the word "may" is therefore inconsistent with respondents' proposed inference from the statutory structure. If Congress had intended section 1225(b)(2)(C) to operate as a mandatory cure of any noncompliance with the Government's detention obligations, it would not have conveyed that intention through an unspoken inference in conflict with the unambiguous, express term "may."*[2]

The Court said that the statute could have been written to impose a mandatory requirement, but it was not and "we will not rewrite it to include one."[3]

The Court also stressed the "foreign affairs consequences" of requiring the government to return all asylum seekers to Mexico while they wait for a hearing. The Court explained that the federal government cannot return asylum seekers to Mexico without the Mexican government's cooperation and requiring the Biden administration to keep the Migrant Protection Protocol in place, Roberts wrote, had "force[d] the Executive to the bargaining table with Mexico, over a policy that both countries wish to terminate. . . . Congress did not intend section 1225(b)(2)(C) to tie the hands of the Executive in this manner."[4]

Justice Alito wrote a dissenting opinion joined by Justices Thomas and Gorsuch. He focused on what he saw as the congressional mandate to keep noncitizens out of the United States. He wrote:

> *In fiscal year 2021, the Border Patrol reported more than 1.7 million encounters with aliens along the Mexican bor-*

> *der. When it appears that one of these aliens is not admissible, may the Government simply release the alien in this country and hope that the alien will show up for the hearing at which his or her entitlement to remain will be decided? Congress has provided a clear answer to that question, and the answer is no.*[5]

Justice Alito said that Congress offered the Executive two—and only two—alternatives to detention. He wrote: "First, if an alien is 'arriving on land' from 'a foreign territory contiguous to the United States,' the Department of Homeland Security (DHS) 'may return the alien to that territory pending a [removal] proceeding.' Second, DHS may release individual aliens on 'parole,' but 'only on a case-by-case basis for urgent humanitarian reasons or a significant public benefit.'"[6] He objected that the Department of Homeland Security is violating this requirement and releasing "into this country untold numbers of aliens who are very likely to be removed if they show up for their removal hearings. This practice violates the clear terms of the law, but the Court looks the other way."[7]

Justice Barrett dissented on narrower grounds. She said that there was an important jurisdictional question and would have remanded the case for the lower courts to consider that before the Supreme Court ruled on it and reached the merits.[8]

This was a rare important case this term in which the liberal justices were in the majority. It also is a case with enormous practical consequences for the lives of many people coming through Mexico to seek asylum in the United States. And it is a strong affirmation of the power of the executive branch over immigration matters.

## *Patel v. Garland*

The issue in *Patel v. Garland* is whether federal courts have jurisdiction to review factual findings made by the executive branch during deportation proceedings.[9] The Court ruled, 5–4, that noncitizens seeking certain forms of discretionary relief under immigration law have no opportunity for judicial review of decisions against them.

In 2007, Pankajkumar Patel, who had entered the United States illegally with his wife Jyostnaben in the 1990s, applied to U.S. Citizenship and Immigration Services (USCIS) for discretionary adjustment of status under 8 U.S.C. 1255, which would have made Patel and his wife lawful permanent residents.[10] Patel's application was denied because he had previously checked a box on a Georgia driver's license application falsely stating that he was a U.S. citizen.

Many years later, the federal government initiated removal proceedings against Patel and his wife. Patel argued before an immigration judge that he had mistakenly checked the "citizen" box on the state application and thus lacked the subjective intent necessary to violate the federal statute. Under Georgia law, Patel was eligible to receive a driver's license, regardless of being a noncitizen. Despite the total lack of improper motive on Patel's part, the immigration judge still held that Patel had purposefully lied and deceived government officials. This meant that Patel failed the threshold requirement for relief, not getting to the second step in the inquiry of whether Patel warranted a favorable exercise of discretion.

Congress has given the Attorney General the power, in §1255, to grant relief from removal in certain circumstances, but federal courts have a limited role in this process.[11] For example, Congress, in §1252(a)(2)(B)(i), has barred judicial review of "any judgment regarding the granting of relief" by the Attorney General in denying discretionary relief.[12] The one exception is cases related to "constitutional claims or questions of law."[13]

The Court held that §1252(a)(2)(B)(i) "prohibits review of *any* judgment *regarding* the granting of relief under §1255 and the other enumerated provisions."[14] Justice Amy Coney Barrett wrote the majority opinion and said that the Court has "repeatedly explained" that "the word 'any' has an expansive meaning."[15] The Court said the use of "regarding" "in a legal context generally has a broadening effect, ensuring that the scope of a provision covers not only its subject but also matters relating to that subject."[16] Therefore, the Court concluded that §1252(a)(2)(B)(i) includes judgments of "whatever kind" and "*relating to* the granting of relief."[17]

The Court explained that §1252(a)(2)(D) creates an exception only for constitutional claims and questions of law, "[a]nd if Congress made such questions an exception, it must have left *something* within the rule. The major remaining category is questions of fact."[18] Therefore, the Court concluded that Congress' intent was to preclude factual findings in such proceedings from judicial review.

Justice Gorsuch wrote a dissenting opinion, joined by Justices Breyer, Sotomayor, and Kagan. He began by discussing the serious consequences of the Court's decision: "Today, the Court holds that a federal bureaucracy can make an obvious factual error, one that will result in an individual's removal from this country, and nothing can be done about it. No court may even hear the case. It is a bold claim promising dire consequences for countless lawful immigrants."[19] He lamented "courts are powerless to correct bureaucratic mistakes like these no matter how grave they may be."[20]

Gorsuch examined the statutory language in detail and argued forcefully that the majority misconstrues it. He also emphasized the human consequences of the Court's decision. Patel, who has lived in the United States for nearly 30 years, now faces deportation because he accidentally checked the wrong box on a driver's license application. Most of all, the dissent was concerned that errors that dramatically affect people's lives will go unreviewed and uncorrected.

## *Garland v. Gonzalez*

May the federal courts grant class-wide injunctive relief requiring bond hearings for detainees held more than 180 days? The Supreme Court, in a 6–3 decision in *Garland v. Gonzalez*, interpreted federal law as precluding this.[21]

Two noncitizens who were being detained by the United States pending removal brought separate suits in federal court and argued that federal law, §1231(a)(6), requires the government to provide bond hearings for detainees after six months of detention. Both federal district courts issued class-wide injunctive relief for detainees held for more than 180 days, finding that they were entitled to bond hearings. The Court, in a 6–3 decision, disagreed and held that class-wide injunctive relief was not permissible under the statute.

Justice Samuel Alito wrote the majority opinion and focused on the language of Section 1252(f)(1), which states, "Regardless of the nature of the action or claim or of the identity of the parties or parties bringing the action, no court (other than the Supreme Court) shall have jurisdiction or authority to enjoin or restrain the operation of [certain INA provisions], other than with respect to the application of such provisions to an individual alien against whom proceedings under such part have been initiated."[22]

Justice Alito focused on how dictionaries define the key words of the statute: "to enjoin," "to restrain," and "operation of."[23] He concluded that this language "generally prohibits lower courts from entering injunctions that order federal officials to take or to refrain from taking actions to *enforce, implement, or otherwise carry out* the specified statutory provisions."[24] He said that the statute thus prohibits injunctions even against illegal executive action. The one exception is for "an individual alien against whom proceedings under such part have been initiated."[25] The result is that any relief must be sought and provided on an individual basis; class-wide injunctive relief is not allowed.

Justice Sotomayor, joined by Breyer and Justice Elena Kagan, dissented, and objected to the majority's use of "piecemeal dictionary definitions and policy concerns over plain meaning and context."[26] Sotomayor emphasized the context of the words within the statute and argued that the jurisdictional provision does not bar lower courts from issuing injunctions that order the executive branch to comply with the law. The dissent argued that the majority ignores Congress' "careful choice of language," disregarding the standard for interpretation of congressional statutory language.[27]

The dissent also argued that lower courts possessed jurisdiction to grant class-wide injunctive relief because each member of the class and beneficiary of the injunction was "an individual alien against whom [removal] proceedings . . . had been initiated."[28] Because the exception to §1252(f)(1) extends only to individual noncitizens, and each class member is certified as an individual noncitizen, the injunction is permissible.

The decision has important implications. By precluding class-wide relief, the Court is requiring that each individual litigate separately. Obtaining counsel is often difficult and frequently impossible in immigration proceedings. The dissent expressed great concern that the result is that many individuals will be denied "a meaningful opportunity to protect their rights."[29]

## *Johnson v. Arteaga-Martinez*

Under federal immigration law, §1231(a)(6), a noncitizen facing prolonged detention is entitled by statute to a bond hearing before an immigration judge and must be released from detention unless the government establishes, by clear and convincing evidence, that the noncitizen poses a risk of flight or a danger to the community.[30] The issue here is whether the government is required to offer detained noncitizens bond hearings after six months of detention under the text of Section 1231(a)(6). The Court held that Section 1231(a)(6) does not require the government to provide noncitizens detained for six months with bond hearings.[31]

In July 2012, Antonio Arteaga-Martinez was removed from the United States. In September 2012, he reentered the country from Mexico. ICE issued a warrant for Arteaga-Martinez's arrest in 2018. ICE reinstated Arteaga-Martinez's previous removal order and detained him pursuant to the Immigration and Nationality Act.[32] Arteaga-Martinez applied for withholding removal under §1231(b)(3) and relief under the Convention Against Torture. He stated that relief was necessary due to fear of persecution or torture he would encounter by returning to Mexico. The Department of Homeland Security referred him to an asylum officer, who affirmed that Arteaga-Martinez demonstrated a reasonable fear of torture.

After being detained for four months, Arteaga-Martinez filed a petition for a writ of habeas corpus in federal district court. He challenged his continued detention on statutory and constitutional grounds. The district court ordered the government to provide him with an individualized bond hearing before an immigration judge and the U.S. Court of Appeals for the Third Circuit affirmed.

The Court, in an 8–1 decision, with Justice Sotomayor writing for the majority, held that the statute did not require a bond hearing. The Court said that the statutory language was clear that no bond hearing was required in these circumstances. But the Court left open the constitutional question of whether due process demanded this. The Court explained that because the lower courts focused entirely on the statutory authority, the constitutional issue was not properly before the justices. It is an issue that the Court has left open on a number of occasions and will soon need to resolve.

## Conclusions

It is worth noting that the U.S. government prevailed in all four immigration cases. This reflects the continuing deference by the Supreme Court to the federal government in immigration matters. But there also is a significant difference among them. *Biden v. Texas* is a victory for those seeking asylum in the United States who under the Trump policy were required to remain indefinitely in Mexico. The other three cases were clear losses for noncitizens seeking relief in the federal courts.

## Endnotes

1. 142 S. Ct. 2528 (2022).
2. *Id.* at 2541 (internal citations omitted).
3. *Id.* (internal citations omitted).
4. *Id.* at 2543.
5. *Id.* at 2549 (Alito, J., dissenting) (footnote omitted).
6. *Id.* at 2550 (internal citations omitted).
7. *Id.*
8. *Id.* at 2560 (Barrett, J., dissenting).
9. 142 S. Ct. 1614 (2022).
10. *Id.* at 1615.
11. 8 U.S.C §1255.
12. §1252(a)(2)(B)(i).
13. 8 U.S.C. §1252(a)(2)(D).
14. 142 S. Ct. at 1622.
15. *Id.* (internal quotations omitted).
16. *Id.* (internal quotations omitted).
17. *Id.*
18. *Id.* at 1623.
19. *Id.* at 1627 (Gorsuch, J., dissenting).
20. *Id.* at 1630.
21. 142 S.Ct. 2057.
22. 8 U.S.C. § 1252(f)(1).

23. 142 S. Ct. at 2064.
24. *Id.* at 2065 (emphasis added).
25. *Id.* (quoting 8 U.S.C. § 1252(f)(1)) .
26. *Id.* at 2068 (Sotomayor, J., dissenting).
27. *Id.* at 2070.
28. *Id.*at 2072 (quoting 8 U.S.C. § 1252(f)(1)).
29. *Id.* at 2076.
30. *See Guerrero-Sanchez* v. *Warden York County Prison*, 905 F. 3d 208, 224 (2018).
31. Johnson v. Arteaga-Martinez, 142 S. Ct. 1827, 1830 (2022).
32. *See* 8 U. S. C. §1231(a).

# 11

# Indian Law

In 2020, the Court decided the landmark case of *McGirt v. Oklahoma* and held that pursuant to the Major Crimes Act and a treaty between the United States and the Creek Nation, members of that tribe who commit crimes on Indian country cannot be prosecuted in state court.[1] The decision was 5–4, with Justice Neil Gorsuch writing the majority opinion, which was joined by Justices Ginsburg, Breyer, Sotomayor, and Kagan. The effect of the decision is that a significant part of Oklahoma is deemed Indian country.

The issue this term, in *Oklahoma v. Castro-Huerta*, was whether a nontribal member could be prosecuted in state court for crimes committed against a tribal member in Indian country.[2] The Court, 5–4, ruled that such cases can be brought in state court, with Justice Kavanaugh writing the opinion, joined by Chief Justice Roberts and Justices Thomas, Alito, and Barrett.

Of course, there is a difference in the issue between the two cases. But the real distinction is in the composition of the Court, with Justice Ginsburg having been replaced by Justice Barrett. There is thus a strong sense that *McGirt* would not be decided the same way today and that, of course, raises speculation of whether the five in the majority in *Castro-Huerta* may want to reconsider *McGirt*. But it also is possible that the decision in *Castro-Huerta*, which limits the number of cases that must be litigated in federal court and that cannot be prosecuted in state court, may lessen the pressure on the Court to overrule *McGirt.*

## *McGirt v. Oklahoma*

The Major Crimes Act provides that, within "the Indian country," "[a]ny Indian who commits" certain enumerated offenses "shall be subject to the same law and penalties as all other persons committing any of [those] offenses, within the exclusive jurisdiction of the United States."[3] "Indian country" includes "all land within the limits of any Indian reservation under the jurisdiction of the United States Government."[4] Under this law, the tribes retain jurisdiction to try individuals for crimes in Indian country and the federal government has authority to try certain crimes, but as the Court noted: "State courts generally have no jurisdiction to try Indians for conduct committed in 'Indian country.'"[5]

Jimcy McGirt was convicted in 1997 by an Oklahoma state court of molesting, raping, and forcibly sodomizing a four-year-old girl, his wife's granddaughter. McGirt was sentenced to 1,000 years plus life in prison.

He argued to the Supreme Court that the state lacked jurisdiction to prosecute him because he is an enrolled member of the Seminole Nation and his crimes took place on the Creek Reservation. The Supreme Court said that the crucial question was whether his crimes occurred in "Indian country." The Supreme Court, in a 5–4 decision, held that for purposes of the Major Crimes Act, land reserved for the Creek Nation since the 19th century remains "Indian country." Justice Gorsuch focused on acts of Congress and said that Congress had never disestablished the Native American reservation. Therefore McGirt, as a tribal member, could not be tried in state court for crimes committed on tribal land.

Justice Gorsuch concluded his majority opinion by declaring:

> *The federal government promised the Creek a reservation in perpetuity. Over time, Congress has diminished that reservation. It has sometimes restricted and other times expanded the Tribe's authority. But Congress has never withdrawn the*

> *promised reservation. As a result, many of the arguments before us today follow a sadly familiar pattern. Yes, promises were made, but the price of keeping them has become too great, so now we should just cast a blind eye. We reject that thinking. If Congress wishes to withdraw its promises, it must say so. Unlawful acts, performed long enough and with sufficient vigor, are never enough to amend the law. To hold otherwise would be to elevate the most brazen and longstanding injustices over the law, both rewarding wrong and failing those in the right.*[6]

Chief Justice Roberts, writing for the four dissenters, emphatically disagreed with the majority that the crime occurred on Indian land. He said that the treaties that would have made it Indian country were no longer in effect. Most of all, he expressed great concern about the implications of the decision. He wrote: "Today, the Court holds that Oklahoma lacked jurisdiction to prosecute McGirt—on the improbable ground that, unbeknownst to anyone for the past century, a huge swathe of Oklahoma is actually a Creek Indian reservation, on which the State may not prosecute serious crimes committed by Indians like McGirt."[7] The dissent described the vast area covered: the Creek reservation, by the majority's analysis, covers 3 million acres and additional reservations would cover 19 million acres.

The dissent complained:

> *Across this vast area, the State's ability to prosecute serious crimes will be hobbled and decades of past convictions could well be thrown out. On top of that, the Court has profoundly destabilized the governance of eastern Oklahoma. The decision today creates significant uncertainty for the State's continuing authority over any area that touches Indian affairs, ranging from zoning and taxation to family and environmental law. None of this is warranted. What has gone unquestioned for a century remains true today: A huge portion of Oklahoma is not a Creek Indian reservation. Congress disestablished any reser-*

> *vation in a series of statutes leading up to Oklahoma statehood at the turn of the 19th century.*[8]

There have been many petitions for certiorari by the State of Oklahoma asking the Court to reconsider and overrule *McGirt*. None have been granted.

## *Oklahoma v. Castro-Huerta*

Victor Manuel Castro-Huerta lived in Tulsa, Oklahoma, with his wife and their several children, including Castro-Huerta's then-five-year-old stepdaughter, who is a Cherokee Indian. Castro-Huerta, who is not a tribal member, was accused of severely neglecting his stepdaughter. He was convicted and sentenced to 35 years of imprisonment.

Under the Court's decision in *McGirt*, the crimes occurred in Indian country. Castro-Huerta, relying on *McGirt*, argued that the state court lacked jurisdiction to try and convict him. The Supreme Court rejected this argument and held that a state has concurrent jurisdiction with the federal government to prosecute crimes committed by non-Indians against Indians in Indian country. Justice Kavanaugh wrote for the Court in a 5–4 decision and said that "the Court's precedents establish that Indian country is part of a State's territory and that, unless preempted, States have jurisdiction over crimes committed in Indian country."[9]

Castro-Huerta relied on the General Crimes Act, which provides: "Except as otherwise expressly provided by law, the general laws of the United States as to the punishment of offenses committed in any place within the sole and exclusive jurisdiction of the United States, except the District of Columbia, shall extend to the Indian country."[10] Castro-Huerta said that this statutory language precluded his prosecution in state court. But the Court rejected this argument and said,

> *By its terms, the Act does not preempt the State's authority to prosecute non-Indians who commit crimes against Indians in Indian country. . . . Importantly, however, the General Crimes Act does not say that Indian country is equivalent to a federal*

*enclave for jurisdictional purposes. Nor does the Act say that federal jurisdiction is exclusive in Indian country, or that state jurisdiction is preempted in Indian country.*[11]

Justice Kavanaugh stressed that "the General Crimes Act does not treat Indian country as the equivalent of a federal enclave for jurisdictional purposes. Nor does the Act make federal jurisdiction exclusive or preempt state law in Indian country."[12] After reviewing other sources of law, the Court concluded that state courts have concurrent jurisdiction for crimes by nontribal members committed in Indian country.

Justice Gorsuch, writing for himself and the three liberal justices, stressed the history of terrible mistreatment of American Indians.[13] The dissent saw this case as taking important authority away from Native American tribes. Justice Gorsuch wrote: "The real party in interest here isn't Mr. Castro-Huerta but the Cherokee, a Tribe of 400,000 members with its own government. Yet the Cherokee have no voice as parties in these proceedings; they and other Tribes are relegated to the filing of *amicus* briefs."[14]

Justice Gorsuch identified what he saw as the errors of the majority's reasoning:

*First, tribal sovereign authority excludes the operation of other sovereigns' criminal laws unless and until Congress ordains otherwise. Second, while Congress has extended a good deal of federal criminal law to tribal lands, in Oklahoma it has authorized the State to prosecute crimes by or against Native Americans within tribal boundaries only if it satisfies certain requirements. Under Public Law 280, the State must remove state-law barriers to jurisdiction and obtain tribal consent. Third, because Oklahoma has done neither of these things, it lacks the authority it seeks to try crimes against tribal members within a tribal reservation. Until today, all this settled law was well appreciated by this Court, the Executive Branch, and even Oklahoma.*[15]

For the dissent, the majority was removing an important attribute of tribal sovereignty by recognizing concurrent jurisdiction in state courts.

## Implications

All four dissenters from *McGirt* are in the majority in *Castro-Huerta* and are joined by Justice Barrett. All four from the majority in *McGirt* are in dissent in *Castro-Huerta*; the fifth member of the *McGirt* majority was Justice Ginsburg.

Interestingly, Oklahoma asked the Court to consider the question of whether *McGirt* should be overruled. The Court did not take that issue. Yet Justice Kavanaugh, in the majority opinion, stressed the burdens *McGirt* is creating for Oklahoma and the federal courts. He wrote:

> *The Oklahoma courts have reversed numerous state convictions on that same jurisdictional ground. After having their state convictions reversed, some non-Indian criminals have received lighter sentences in plea deals negotiated with the Federal Government. Others have simply gone free. Going forward, the State estimates that it will have to transfer prosecutorial responsibility for more than 18,000 cases per year to the Federal and Tribal Governments. All of this has created a significant challenge for the Federal Government and for the people of Oklahoma. . . . And the Department recently acknowledged that "many people may not be held accountable for their criminal conduct due to resource constraints."*[16]

This suggests that the majority in *Castro-Huerta* may be willing to reconsider *McGirt*. But it hasn't happened yet. *Castro-Huerta* distinguishes and limits the reach of *McGirth*, but it does not in any way overrule it.

## Endnotes

1. 140 S. Ct. 2452 (2020).
2. 142 S. Ct. 2486 (2022).
3. 18 U.S.C. § 1153(a).
4. § 1151.
5. 140 S. Ct. at 2459.

6. *Id.* at 2482.
7. *Id.* at 2482 (Roberts, C.J., dissenting).
8. *Id.*
9. 142 S. Ct. 2496 (2022).
10. 18 U.S.C. § 1152.
11. 142 S. Ct. at 2495.
12. *Id.* at 2496.
13. There is an interesting difference in the choice of language between the majority and the dissent. Justice Gorsuch, in dissent, primarily refers to "Native Americans." Justice Kavanaugh's majority opinion never once uses that phrase, referring instead to Indians.
14. *Id.* at 2510-2511 (Gorsuch, J., dissenting).
15. *Id.* at 2518.
16. 142 S. Ct. at 2492 (internal citations omitted).

12

# The Second Amendment

It was no surprise that the Supreme Court declared unconstitutional the New York law limiting concealed weapons in public. Given the ideological composition of the Court and the tenor of the oral argument in the case, that result was expected. The surprise was how the Court did this, providing greater protection for Second Amendment rights than virtually any other in the Constitution. Although the actual holding was narrow in *New York State Rifle and Pistol Association v. Bruen*, the approach to Second Amendment cases prescribed by the Court will have enormous implications for gun regulation in the United States.[1]

## The History of the Second Amendment in the Supreme Court

The Second Amendment says, "A well regulated Militia, being necessary to the security of a free State, the right of the people to keep and bear Arms, shall not be infringed." From 1791 until 2008, the Supreme Court never once declared unconstitutional any law—federal, state, or local—as violating the Second Amendment. In the handful of cases about the provision, the Court said that it was just about a right to have guns for militia service.[2]

In June 2008, in *District of Columbia v. Heller*, the Court for the first time declared a gun regulation unconstitutional and struck down a 32-year-old District of Columbia ordinance that prohibited ownership or possession of handguns.[3] The decision was ideologically split, 5–4, with Justice Antonin Scalia writing the opinion for the Court. He said that the first half of the Second Amendment, about militias, was the "prefatory clause," and the latter half was its operative clause protecting a right of the people to keep and bear arms. He said that a prefatory clause cannot limit the meaning of an operative clause.

Justice Scalia traced the history of gun rights in England and the states prior to the ratification of the Constitution. He said: "We therefore believe that the most likely reading of all four of these pre-Second Amendment state constitutional provisions is that they secured an individual right to bear arms for defensive purposes."[4] Justice Scalia then looked at the post-ratification commentary, the pre-Civil War cases, the post-Civil War legislation and cases, and said that all of these confirm that the Second Amendment was not meant to be limited to a right to have firearms for militia service.

The Court held that the Second Amendment protects a right to have guns in the home for the sake of security. The Court did not prescribe a level of scrutiny but made clear that the Second Amendment is not absolute. The Court said that the government can regulate who has guns, such as keeping those with a felony conviction or history of serious mental illness from having guns. Also, the government can limit where people have guns, such as prohibiting them near schools or public places. And the government can prevent people from having especially dangerous weapons.[5]

Two years later, in *McDonald v. City of Chicago* (2010), the Supreme Court held, again 5–4, that the Second Amendment applies to state and local governments.[6] Because the District of Columbia is a part of the federal government, it took a separate decision to hold that the Second Amendment is incorporated into the due process clause of the Fourteenth Amendment and applies to state and local governments.

## *New York State Rifle and Pistol Association v. Bruen*

There were no Supreme Court decisions about the Second Amendment for the last twelve years, a time during which the composition of the Court changed greatly and became much more conservative. *New York State Rifle and Pistol Association v. Bruen* involves a New York law, initially adopted in 1911, that prohibits having weapons in public without a permit. If a person wants to carry a firearm outside the home or place of business for self-defense, the applicant must obtain an unrestricted license to "have and carry" a concealed "pistol or revolver." To secure that license, the applicant must prove that "proper cause exists" to issue it. New York courts have interpreted this to require that a person "demonstrate a special need for self-protection distinguishable from that of the general community."

The Court noted that New York was one of six states that has a law requiring that a person demonstrate a need for a concealed weapon in order to have a permit allowing this in public. By contrast, 43 states have laws that the Court described as "shall issue" jurisdictions, "where authorities must issue concealed-carry licenses whenever applicants satisfy certain threshold requirements, without granting licensing officials discretion to deny licenses based on a perceived lack of need or suitability."

In a 6–3 decision, with the majority opinion written by Justice Clarence Thomas, the Court declared the New York law unconstitutional. For the first time in American history, the Court was explicit that "the Second and Fourteenth Amendments protect an individual's right to carry a handgun for self-defense outside the home."[7] The Court held that state laws are unconstitutional if they restrict having concealed weapons to those who show cause.

Justice Kavanaugh, in a concurring opinion, said that this is all the Court held.[8] But Justice Thomas's opinion, which was joined by five justices, including Kavanaugh, went much further in specifying when the government can regulate guns.

Most Circuits had adopted a two-step approach to evaluating gun restrictions. At the first step, the government could justify a regulation of firearms by "establish[ing] that the challenged law regulates activity falling outside the scope of the right as originally understood."[9] But if the historical evidence is "inconclusive or suggests that the regulated activity is *not* categorically unprotected," courts would proceed to step two and analyze "how close the law comes to the core of the Second Amendment right and the severity of the law's burden on that right." Many characterized this as a form of intermediate scrutiny.

The Court in Justice Thomas's opinion expressly rejected this and said, "we decline to adopt that two-part approach."[10] The Court said that judges applying it and intermediate scrutiny have given too much deference to legislative regulation of guns.

When the Court deems a right fundamental and wants more than intermediate scrutiny, it adopts strict scrutiny, requiring that the government action be necessary to achieve a compelling interest. But that is not what the Court did in *Bruen*. Instead, the Court said that a gun regulation is constitutionally permissible *only* if it was historically allowed. The Court declared:

> *To justify its regulation, the government may not simply posit that the regulation promotes an important interest. Rather, the government must demonstrate that the regulation is consistent with this Nation's historical tradition of firearm regulation. Only if a firearm regulation is consistent with this Nation's historical tradition may a court conclude that the individual's conduct falls outside the Second Amendment's "unqualified command."*[11]

The Court expressly rejected any balancing of the government's interests in regulating guns with a claim of Second Amendment rights. Justice Thomas wrote "the Second Amendment is the very product of an interest balancing by the people and *it surely elevates above all other interests* the right of law-abiding, responsible citizens to use arms for self-defense."[12] The Court said that it was rejecting any analysis of means and ends, such as whether the government regulation serves a compelling interest and whether it is necessary to achieve it.

Several times in the majority opinion, the Court stressed that government regulation of guns is allowed only if it was historically permitted. The Court was unclear, and Justice Barrett raised this in a concurring opinion,[13] as to how to determine what was historically done and whether the focus should only look at what was allowed in 1791 or whether it also should look to practices in 1868 when the Fourteenth Amendment was adopted.

Justice Thomas said that from either perspective the New York law is unconstitutional. He undertook a detailed review of the history of regulating concealed weapons in public and concluded that it did not support the New York law.

The Court gave relatively little guidance as to how this historical analysis is to be done.

The Court was clear, though, that the Second Amendment is not limited to protecting only the types of weapons that existed in 1791. The Court said that this is similar to how the First Amendment is not limited to protecting only the types of media that existed when the Bill of Rights was adopted. Justice Thomas said that courts must reason by analogy. He wrote:

> *Although its meaning is fixed according to the understandings of those who ratified it, the Constitution can, and must, apply to circumstances beyond those the Founders specifically anticipated. . . . While we do not now provide an exhaustive survey of the features that render regulations relevantly similar under the Second Amendment, we do think that* Heller *and* McDonald *point toward at least two metrics: how and why the regulations burden a law-abiding citizen's right to armed self-defense. As we stated in* Heller *and repeated in* McDonald, *"individual self-defense is the central component'" of the Second Amendment right.*[14]

## The Dissent

Justice Breyer wrote the dissenting opinion joined by Justices Sotomayor and Kagan. He began by describing the problem of gun violence in the United States: "In 2020, 45,222 Americans were killed by firearms. Since the start of this year (2022), there have been 277 reported mass shootings—an average of more than one per day."[15] He pointed to studies that laws, like New York's, limiting concealed weapons in public make a difference in reducing gun deaths. For example, a study that examined the 33 states that adopted laws requiring issuance of concealed weapons permits between 1981 and 2007 found that the "adoption of those laws was associated with a 13%–15% increase in rates of violent crime after 10 years."[16]

The dissent criticized the refusal of the majority to apply even strict scrutiny. Justice Breyer wrote: "it refuses to consider whether New York has a compelling interest in regulating the concealed carriage of handguns or whether New York's law is narrowly tailored to achieve that interest. Although I agree that history can often be a useful tool in determining the meaning and scope of constitutional provisions, I believe the Court's near-exclusive reliance on that single tool today goes much too far."[17]

The dissent argued that history is often unclear, with inconsistent traditions and practices. Justice Breyer questioned whether lower courts have the resources needed for extensive historical research and whether lawyers and judges have the training as historians to do so. He recited at length the long history of regulating concealed weapons, which would support the New York law. He lamented that the Court "gives the lower courts precious little guidance regarding how to resolve modern constitutional questions based almost solely on history."[18] He stressed "that history will be an especially inadequate tool when it comes to modern cases presenting modern problems."[19]

## Implications

*New York State Rifle and Pistol Association v. Bruen* is, by far, the most expansive reading of the Second Amendment in American history and its approach will put countless laws regulating firearms in serious jeopardy.

First, the case is significant in holding, for the first time, that the Second Amendment protects a right to have guns in public. Second, the decision is important in ruling that this includes a right to have concealed weapons. The Court said that laws that require a concealed weapons permit are constitutional so long as they have clear criteria leaving no discretion to the licensing authority. Laws that limit having a concealed weapon to those who show "cause" and give discretion to licensing officials are unconstitutional.

Third, and most important for future litigation, the Court rejects using the levels of scrutiny, including strict scrutiny. In most areas of constitutional law when there is a fundamental right—such as freedom of speech, free exercise of religion, protection from race discrimination—the Court has said that the government may act if it meets strict scrutiny. But the Court in *Bruen* said this is not the approach for the Second Amendment. The Court was emphatic that the only relevant inquiry in considering the constitutionality of a gun regulation is whether it was historically allowed:

> *We reiterate that the standard for applying the Second Amendment is as follows: When the Second Amendment's plain text covers an individual's conduct, the Constitution presumptively protects that conduct. The government must then justify its regulation by demonstrating that it is consistent with the Nation's historical tradition of firearm regulation. Only then may a court conclude that the individual's conduct falls outside the Second Amendment's "unqualified command."*[20]

This is unique in constitutional law and provides more protection for Second Amendment rights than any other. The government can interfere with other fundamental rights if strict scrutiny is met, but not so for the Second Amendment. Gun regulations are permissible only if it can be shown that they were historically allowed. And the primary focus is on what was done in 1791, when the Second Amendment was enacted, or 1868, when the Fourteenth Amendment was ratified.

This means that litigants and judges in lower courts will need to immerse themselves in history. Of course, history is often unclear. In *Bruen*, both Justice Thomas in the majority opinion and Justice Breyer in dissent looked exhaustively at history—from English law to that in the colonies to after ratification of the Constitution to the time of the adoption of the Fourteenth Amendment to later experiences—and came to exactly opposite conclusions. Also, it will be unclear about how to apply history to types of weapons and problems that had no analogue in 1791 or 1868.

It is important to recognize that this is a different, and more expansive, use of originalism than ever before from the Supreme Court. Up until now, originalists have used that method of interpretation to define the scope of rights. They have said that a constitutional provision means the same things today as when it was adopted and a right exists only if it is in the text or part of its original meaning. From this perspective, the Second Amendment means the same thing in 2022 as in 1791. But never before has the Court said that once it is determined that there is a right, the scope of regulation is determined by originalism as well. In other words, originalism now is used both to determine whether a right exists *and* to decide whether a government action limiting it is constitutional. All six conservative justices signed on to this emphatic use of originalism.

The Court, though, also was clear that the Second Amendment is not absolute. The example in the majority opinion is the right to regulate guns in sensitive places, like near schools and in public buildings. I am sure the Court would uphold a prohibition of guns in and near courthouses. Justice Kavanaugh, in his concurring opinion, made clear that the Court was not calling into question licensing systems.[21]

But countless gun regulations—federal, state, and local—now will be challenged and the question for each will be whether it was of a type that was historically allowed. It seems that it will be irrelevant whether the government can show a compelling interest for the regulation and even that there is no other way to achieve it. Recall, the Court said "[t]he Second Amendment . . . *surely elevates above all other interests* the right of law-abiding, responsible citizens to use arms for self-defense."[22] Never has the Court said that the Constitution elevates freedom of speech or free exercise of religion or the right to be free from unreasonable searches and seizes "above all other interests."

The disagreement between the majority and the dissent is profound. In part, it reflects the dispute between liberals and conservatives in American society over gun rights. Liberals overall favor gun regulation, pointing, as Justice Breyer does, to the extent of gun violence and gun deaths in the United States. Conservatives, by contrast, favor gun rights, arguing for the need for individuals to have weapons for self-defense.

There also is a disagreement over constitutional interpretation. Justice Thomas's opinion is emphatic in its originalist approach to the Constitution. For an originalist, current public needs are irrelevant. But the liberal justices reject originalism, they favor a living Constitution, and stress the importance of modern needs. It is not surprising that Justice Breyer begins his opinion by talking about the problem of gun violence and mass shootings, while Justice Thomas and Justice Alito in a concurring opinion deem this irrelevant.[23]

And all of this leads to a complete disagreement over who should decide whether gun regulations are allowed. The Court's majority, its six conservative justices, see it as the role of the judiciary to enforce the Second Amendment and to declare unconstitutional laws that infringe it. But the dissenters, the three liberal justices, see this as a matter for the legislature and the political process.

The one certainty is that the Court's decision in *Bruen* will lead to a tremendous amount of litigation challenging gun regulations and that it will make it more difficult for courts to uphold laws, even long-standing ones. The New York statute struck down in *Bruen* was adopted in 1911.

It was 14 years between *Heller* and *Bruen*. Like in every area this term, the change in the composition of the Court—and especially the three justices appointed by President Trump—have made all the difference in moving the law much further to the right.

## Endnotes

1. 142 S. Ct. 2111 (2022).
2. *See, e.g., United States v. Miller*, 307 U.S. 174 (1939); *Presser v. Illinois.*, 116 U.S. 252 (1886); *United States v. Cruikshank*, 92 U.S. 542 (1875).
3. 554 U.S. 570 (2008).
4. *Id.* at 602.
5. *Id.* at 626-27.
6. 561 U.S. 742 (2010).
7. 142 S. Ct. 2122 (2022).
8. Id. at 2161 (Kavanaugh, J., concurring).
9. Quoted in Thomas opinion, 142 S. Ct. at 2126.
10. *Id.*
11. *Id.*
12. *Id.* at 2118 (emphasis added) (quoting *Heller*, 554 U.S. at 635).
13. *Id.* at 2163 (Barrett, J., concurring).

14. *Id.* at 2132-33(internal quotation marks omitted).
15. *Id.* at 2163 (Breyer, J., dissenting).
16. *Id.* at 2173.
17. *Id.* at 2174.
18. *Id.* at 2179.
19. *Id.* at 2180.
20. *Id.* at 2129-30.
21. *Id.* at 2161 (Kavanaugh, J. concurring).
22. *Id.* at 2131 (emphasis added) (internal quotation marks omitted).
23. *Id.* at 2157 (Alito, J., concurring).

13

# The State Secrets Doctrine

## What Is the State Secrets Doctrine?

In the first week of March, the Supreme Court issued two decisions, which expand the "state secrets privilege" and make it harder to expose government misconduct. The state secrets privilege broadly permits the government to prevent disclosure of information that it believes would harm national security interests.

The state secrets privilege was created by the Supreme Court in *United States v. Reynolds* in 1953.[1] It is not found in any statute or Federal Rule of Civil Procedure or Evidence. Although there certainly are instances in which the government needs to protect secrecy for the sake of national security, all too often it has been used to hide government wrongdoing.

### *United States v. Zubaydah*

Both of the recent Supreme Court decisions reversed Ninth Circuit rulings that imposed limits on the state secrets doctrine. *United States v.*

*Zubaydah* held that the state secrets doctrine applies even as to information that already is public and even if it relates to events that are almost 20 years old.[2]

Abu Zubaydah, who remains a prisoner in Guantanamo, alleges that he was held in Poland in 2002 and 2003 where he was tortured. A congressional report documented that he was subjected to more than 80 waterboarding sessions, hundreds of hours of live burial, and forced rectal feeding and hydration.[3]

Zubaydah has a lawsuit pending in Poland against those who he said were responsible for his torture. He filed an action in federal district court seeking to subpoena two former Central Intelligence Agency contractors. The government invoked the state secrets doctrine, claiming that Zubaydah's discovery request could force former CIA contractors to confirm the location of the detention site and that confirmation would itself significantly harm national security interests.

The U.S. Court of Appeals for the Ninth Circuit rejected the government's argument, explaining that the site's location had already been publicly disclosed.[4] The torture of Zubaydah and others at the site has been well documented, including in the Executive Summary of a Senate Select Committee on Intelligence Report and by the European Court of Human Rights' findings.[5] The Ninth Circuit said the state secrets privilege did not bar disclosure of information that was no longer secret and which was being sought from private parties.

But the Supreme Court reversed and ordered Zubaydah's case dismissed. The decision was 7–2, with Justice Stephen Breyer writing for the majority. The Court said that releasing the information would necessarily tend to confirm (or deny) that the CIA maintained a detention site in Poland. The Court accepted the government's claim that such information—even if already made public through unofficial sources—could significantly harm national security. The Court declared: "We agree with the Government that sometimes information that has entered the public domain may nonetheless fall within the scope of the state secrets privilege. The Government here has provided a reasonable explanation of why Mitchell and Jessen's confirmation or denial of the information Zubaydah seeks could significantly harm national security interests, even if that information has already been made public through unofficial sources."[6] The Court expressly rejected the Ninth Circuit's view that "in order to be a 'state secret,' a fact must first be a 'secret.'"

The dissent expressed concern that this is about what the government did almost 20 years ago and it is information that already is public from a variety of sources, including congressional reports. Most importantly, the dissent argued that if the U.S. government participated in torture, then this should be made public. Justice Neil Gorsuch, in a dissent joined by Justice Sonia Sotomayor, powerfully declared:

> *There comes a point where we should not be ignorant as judges of what we know to be true as citizens. This case takes us well past that point. Zubaydah seeks information about his torture at the hands of the CIA. The events in question took place two decades ago. They have long been declassified. Official reports have been published, books written, and movies made about them. Still, the government seeks to have this suit dismissed on the ground it implicates a state secret—and today the Court acquiesces in that request. Ending this suit may shield the government from some further modest measure of embarrassment. But respectfully, we should not pretend it will safeguard any secret.*[7]

## *Federal Bureau of Investigation v. Fazaga*

The next day, the Court again broadened the state secrets privilege in *Federal Bureau of Investigation v. Fazaga.*[8] Yassir Fazaga, Ali Malik, and Yasser Abdel Rahim are members of Muslim communities in southern California who claim that the Federal Bureau of Investigation illegally surveilled them because of their religion. The plaintiffs sued under the Foreign Intelligence Surveillance Act, which limits electronic surveillance by the government and authorizes civil suits. The Ninth Circuit ruled that "Congress intended FISA to displace the state secrets privilege and its dismissal remedy with respect to electronic surveillance."[9] The Ninth Circuit reasoned that, under well-established legal principles, statutes can override common law privileges.

But the Supreme Court unanimously reversed in an opinion by Justice Samuel Alito. The Court explained: "FISA makes no reference to the state secrets privilege. . . . The absence of any statutory reference to the state secrets privilege is strong evidence that the availability of the privilege was not altered in any way. Regardless of whether the state secrets privilege is rooted only in the common law (as respondents argue) or also in the Constitution (as the Government argues), the privilege should not be held to have been abrogated or limited unless Congress has at least used clear statutory language."[10]

## Implications

Both of these cases make it easier for the government to use the state secrets privilege to hide its misconduct. In fact, the United States has consistently been able to use this doctrine to escape being held liable for its torture during the war on terrorism.

For example, in *El-Masri v. United States*, in 2007, the U.S. Court of Appeals for the Fourth Circuit dismissed a lawsuit by a man who had been brutally tortured because of mistaken identity.[11] Khaled El-Masri sued federal government officials who he claimed were responsible for him being abducted, imprisoned for 23 days in a CIA-operated detention facility in Afghanistan, drugged, and tortured. He was released and dumped on the streets of Albania when it was discovered that it was a case of mistaken identity; he was confused with someone with the same name. Although his torture was widely reported, including in Jane Mayer's book, *The Dark Side*,[12] the U.S. Court of Appeals for the Fourth Circuit said that his case had to be dismissed because of the state secrets privilege.

Similarly, in *Mohamed v. Jeppesen Dataplan, Inc.*, in 2010, the U.S. Court of Appeals for the Ninth Circuit dismissed a claim against a company that transported individuals to detention sites where they were tortured.[13] One of the plaintiffs described being subjected to "severe physical and psychological torture," including the CIA routinely beating him and breaking his bones. He says he was cut with a scalpel all over his body, including on his penis, and "hot stinging liquid" was poured into the open wounds. He was held in Guantanamo for five years and then released, having never been tried or convicted of anything. But the Court of Appeals dismissed the suits by him and others who received similar treatment based on the state secrets doctrine.

Long ago, James Madison wrote, "[a] popular Government, without popular information, or the means of acquiring it, is but a Prologue to a Farce or a Tragedy; or, perhaps, both. Knowledge will forever govern ignorance: And a people who mean to be their own Governors, must arm themselves with the power which knowledge gives."[14] Unfortunately, the Supreme Court's two recent decisions make it much harder to have knowledge about our government's misconduct.

## Endnotes

1. 345 U.S. 1 (1953). For an excellent discussion of this case, *see* Barry Siegel, Claim of Privilege: A Mysterious Plane Crash, a Landmark Supreme Court Case, and the Rise of State Secrets (2008).
2. 142 S. Ct. 959 (2022).
3. *Id.* at 986 (Gorsuch, J., dissenting).
4. *Id.* at 964 (referencing Husayn v. Mitchell, 938 F.3d 1123, 1132–34 (2019)).
5. *Id.* at 964–65; *see also id.* at 986–987 (Gorsuch, J., dissenting). *See, e.g.*, United States. S. Rep. No. 288, 113th Cong., 2d Sess. (2014) (SSCI Report); Husayn (Abu Zubaydah) v. Poland, no. 7511/13, ¶¶ 404–529, ECHR 2014.
6. 142 S. Ct. at 968 (internal citations omitted)..
7. *Id.* at 985(Gorsuch, J., dissenting) (internal citations omitted).
8. 142 S. Ct. 1051 (2022).
9. Fazaga v. Fed. Bureau of Investigation, 965 F.3d 1015, 1052 (2020).
10. 142 S. Ct. at 1060–61.
11. 479 F.3d 296 (2007).
12. Jane Mayer, The Dark Side: The Inside Story of How the War on Terror Turned Into a War on American Ideals (2009).
13. 614 F.3d 1070 (2010).
14. James Madison, Letter from James Madison to W.T. Barry (August 4, 1822), *in* The Writings of James Madison Volume IX 103, 103 (Gaillard Hunt ed., 1900).

14

# Conclusion: Looking Ahead

I do not think that anyone, liberal or conservative, would deny that October 2021 was a momentous term in the Supreme Court. But it would be a mistake to see this as an aberration rather than as a harbinger of what is to come. The Court continues to have six conservative justices and three liberal justices, even with the addition of Justice Ketanji Brown Jackson.

The reality is that these conservative justices would have decided countless cases differently if they had been on the bench over the last half century. They have shown that they are willing to overrule precedents. We obviously saw the effects of this in October 2021, most notably in the Court overruling *Roe v. Wade* and *Lemon v. Kurtzman*. What might we see next term and in the years to come?

## October Term 2022

Traditionally about half the docket is set before the justices go on their summer recess. The Court continues to take cases that will be argued this term from the end of September until mid-January. Already there are a number of potential blockbusters.

**Affirmative Action.** In a series of cases over more than four decades, the Supreme Court has held that colleges and universities have a compelling interest in having a diverse student body and may use race as one factor in admissions to benefit minorities and to enhance diversity. This was initially articulated by Justice Lewis Powell in *Regents of the University of California v. Bakke* in 1978,[1] was the holding of the majority in *Grutter v. Bollinger* in 2003,[2] and was reaffirmed in *Fisher v. University of Texas, Austin* in 2016.[3]

But two of the justices who were in the majority in *Fisher*—Justices Anthony Kennedy and Ruth Bader Ginsburg—are no longer on the Court. All three dissenters from *Fisher*—Chief Justice Roberts and Justices Thomas and Alito—remain. Three additional conservatives—Justices Gorsuch, Kavanaugh, and Barrett—now are on the bench.

The Court will hear two cases in October Term 2022 that pose the question of whether the Court should overrule *Bakke*, *Grutter*, and *Fisher*: *Students for Fair Admission v. University of North Carolina*[4] and *Students for Fair Admission v. President and Fellows of Harvard College*.[5] By taking both cases, the Court will be ruling on the future of affirmative action in *both* public and private colleges and universities.

As a public university, the University of North Carolina case involves whether affirmative action violates equal protection. Although the Constitution does not apply to a private school, like Harvard, Title VI of the 1964 Civil Rights Act prohibits recipients of federal funds from discriminating based on race. The Court has said that the standard under Title VI is the same as under equal protection.[6] There is thus the real possibility of an end of affirmative action for both public and private higher education in the United States.

**Copyright.** A crucial question that often arises in copyright litigation in determining whether there is "fair use" is whether a work is "transformative." In *Andy Warhol Foundation for the Visual Arts v. Goldsmith*, the Court will consider what it means for a work of art to be "transformative" for purposes of fair use under the Copyright Act.[7] If a work is transformative, it is much more likely to be deemed fair use and thus not a violation of the copyright law. This case involves the artist Andy Warhol and a number of images he created from Lynn Goldsmith's photo of Prince. The Second Circuit ruled that they were not transformative.

The Supreme Court granted review on the question: "Whether a work of art is 'transformative' when it conveys a different meaning or message from its source material (as the Supreme Court, U.S. Court of Appeals for the 9th Circuit, and other courts of appeals have held), or whether a court is forbidden from considering the meaning of the accused work where it 'recognizably deriv[es] from' its source material (as the U.S. Court of Appeals for the 2nd Circuit has held)."[8]

The case is important because this is the first time the Supreme Court has considered the application of fair use to visual art. Visual art fair use cases may be different in the Court's eyes from the music and technology fair use cases that the Court has decided so far.

**Discrimination in Violation of State Law Based on Free Speech (and Free Exercise of Religion).** In *Masterpiece Cakeshop v. Colorado Civil Rights Commission* in 2018, the Court considered whether a business owner, based on his religious beliefs, could discriminate on the basis of sexual orientation.[9]

Charlie Craig and David Mullins got married in Massachusetts and wanted to celebrate their wedding where they lived in Colorado. They went to a local bakery, Masterpiece Cakeshop, a limited liability company in Colorado, and sought to purchase a wedding cake. The owner, Jack Phillips, refused to make the cake, saying that gay marriage violated his religious beliefs.

The Colorado Civil Rights Commission found that Phillips violated Colorado's public accommodations law that prohibits business establishments from discriminating, including on the basis of sexual orientation. Phillips would bake a cake for opposite sex couples, but not for same-sex couples, a form of discrimination that violated state law. The Colorado Court of Appeals affirmed the Commission's ruling against Masterpiece Cake. The Colorado Supreme Court denied review.

The Supreme Court reversed in a 7–2 decision. Justice Kennedy wrote for the Court; only Justices Ginsburg and Sotomayor dissented. The Court did not reach the central issues of the case: would it violate free exercise of religion or freedom of speech under the First Amendment to force Masterpiece Cakeshop to design and bake a cake for a same-sex wedding?

Instead, the Court found that the Colorado Civil Rights Commission had expressed impermissible hostility to religion. Justice Kennedy wrote: "The Civil Rights Commission's treatment of his case has some elements of a clear and impermissible hostility toward the sincere religious beliefs that motivated his objection."[10] The Court found that two members of the Commission had expressed hostility to religion in their comments during deliberations.

The Court returns to this issue in October Term 2022 in *303 Creative LLC v. Elenis*.[11] Lorie Smith owns a graphic design firm and wants to expand her business to include wedding websites. She says that same-sex marriage violates her religious beliefs and does not want to design websites for same-sex weddings. As in *Masterpiece Cakeshop*, Colorado law prohibits such discrimination on the basis of sexual orientation.

The Supreme Court has granted review on the question, "Whether applying a public-accommodation law to compel an artist to speak or stay silent violates the free speech clause of the First Amendment."[12] It is notable that only the free speech question is presented, but obviously religious beliefs underlie this case.

**Elections.** One of the most important cases of the term involves the "independent state legislature" theory. This is the view that under the Constitution, state legislatures control the election of members to Congress and that courts cannot be involved even in enforcing state constitutional requirements. Proponents of this theory point to Article I of the Constitution which says: "The Times, Places and Manner of holding Elections for Senators and Representatives, shall be prescribed in each State by the Legislature thereof; but the Congress may at any time by Law make or alter such Regulations, except as to the Places of choosing Senators."[13] In 2015, in *Arizona State Legislature v. Arizona Redistricting Commission*,[14] the Court, 5–4, rejected that this gives exclusive control to the legislature of a state. But Justices Anthony Kennedy and Ruth Bader Ginsburg were in the majority in that decision and the composition of the Court obviously has changed since then

The case before the Court is *Moore v. Harper*.[15] The North Carolina legislature, controlled by Republicans, drew maps for congressional districts from the state. A challenge was brought in North Carolina state court that the gerrymandering violated the North Carolina Constitution. Although

North Carolina is almost evenly divided politically between Democrats and Republicans, the map would have given Republicans likely control of 10 of 14 congressional districts.

The North Carolina Supreme Court found that the map violated the North Carolina Constitution and enjoined its use. A trial court adopted a new map.

The Supreme Court granted review on the question: "Whether a state's judicial branch may nullify the regulations governing the 'Manner of holding Elections for Senators and Representatives . . . prescribed . . . by the Legislature thereof,' and replace them with regulations of the state courts' own devising, based on vague state constitutional provisions purportedly vesting the state judiciary with power to prescribe whatever rules it deems appropriate to ensure a 'fair' or 'free' election."[16]

On the one hand, proponents of the independent state legislature theory point to the language in the Constitution that gives the power over elections to Congress to state legislatures. On the other hand, a grant of power to the legislature never has been thought to preclude judicial review; Article I of the Constitution empowers Congress, but courts still can declare federal laws unconstitutional. Also, if the Court accepts the independent state legislature theory, there is the crucial question of whether a state, through its constitution or via state laws, can delegate its authority and empower the courts to enforce the state and federal constitutions.

The stakes in this case are enormous. There is another provision of the Constitution which concerns choosing electors for the Electoral College to select the president of the United States. "Each State shall appoint, in such Manner *as the Legislature thereof may direct*, a Number of Electors, equal to the whole Number of Senators and Representatives to which the State may be entitled in the Congress: but no Senator or Representative, or Person holding an Office of Trust or Profit under the United States, shall be appointed an Elector."[17] If the Court were to adopt the independent state legislature theory, then it could conceivably mean that courts would be disempowered to enforce the federal and state constitutions and state laws in presidential elections.

Also, with regard to elections, the Court will hear *Merrill v. Milligan*—discussed in Chapter 6—about the Voting Rights Act.[18] A three-judge federal court found that the map drawn by the Alabama legislature for congressional seats violated Section 2 of the Voting Rights Act. Alabama's population is 27 percent Black, but under the plan, Black voters have the power to elect their preferred candidates in only one of the state's seven congressional districts. The Supreme Court, 5–4, stayed the district court's order and granted review in the case.

**Indian Law.** The Indian Child Welfare Act establishes minimum standards for the removal of Native American children from their families and establishes a preference that Native children who are removed from their families be placed with extended family members or in Native foster homes. The issue in *Haaland v. Brackeen* is whether these provisions of the Indian Child Welfare Act violate the Constitution.[19]

Specifically, the challengers argue that the Act is impermissible commandeering of state courts in violation of the Tenth Amendment. Also, there is the issue of whether equal protection is violated by the preference for placing Native American children with Native American families when there are adoptions or foster care placements.

## The Future

As the Court began October Term 2022, the oldest justice is Clarence Thomas, who turned 74 on June 23. Samuel Alito is 72, while John Roberts is 67. The other three conservative justices are all in their 50s: Brett Kavanaugh is 57, Neil Gorsuch is 55, Amy Coney Barrett is 50.

John Paul Stevens did not retire until he was 90. Ruth Bader Ginsburg was 87 when she died. Stephen Breyer was 83 when he left the Court.

It is thus easy to imagine these six justices being together for another decade or more. And if they can time their retirements for when there is a Republican president to replace them, conservative control of the Court may be secure for a long time to come.

But vacancies are unpredictable and there is no way to know who will be in the White House when they will happen. The Court would be very different today if Justice Ginsburg had retired in 2014 when President Obama could have appointed her successor or if she had lived a few more months so that President Biden would have filled that seat on the Court.

The current Court is very much a product of Donald Trump rather than Hillary Clinton winning the presidency in 2016.

The one safe prediction is that it will be a conservative Court for many years to come and there are likely more momentous terms to follow.

## Endnotes

1. 438 U.S. 265 (1978).
2. 539 U.S. 306 (2003).
3. 579 U.S. 365 (2016).
4. 567 F. Supp. 3d 580 (M.D.N.C. 2021), *cert. granted*, 142 S. Ct. 896 (2022).
5. 980 F.3d 157 (1st Cir. 2020), *cert. granted*, 142 S. Ct. 895 (2022).
6. 539 U.S. at 2430, n.23.
7. 11 F.4th 26 (2d Cir. 2021), *cert. granted*, 142 S. Ct. 1412 (2022).
8. SCOTUSblog, *Andy Warhol Foundation for the Visual Arts, Inc. v. Goldsmith*, SCOTUSblog, https://www.scotusblog.com/case-files/cases/andy-warhol-foundation-for-the-visual-arts-inc-v-goldsmith/.
9. 138 S. Ct. 1719 (2018).
10. *Id.* at 1729.
11. 6 F.4th 1160 (10th Cir. 2021), *cert. granted in part*, 142 S. Ct. 1106 (2022).
12. 142 S. Ct. 1106.
13. U.S. Const. Art. I, § 4, cl. 1.
14. 576 U.S. 787 (2015).
15. Harper v. Hall, 868 S.E.2d 499, *cert. granted sub nom.* Moore v. Harper, No. 21-1271, 2022 WL 2347621 (U.S. June 30, 2022).
16. SCOTUSblog, Moore v. Harper, SCOTUSblog, https://www.scotusblog.com/case-files/cases/moore-v-harper-2/.
17. U.S. Const. Art. 2, § 1, cl. 2 (emphasis added).
18. Singleton v. Merrill, No. 2:21-CV-1291-AMM, 2022 WL 265001, at *2 (N.D. Ala. Jan. 24, 2022), *cert. granted before judgment sub nom.* Merrill v. Milligan 142 S. Ct. 879 (2022).
19. Brackeen v. Haaland, 994 F.3d 249 (5th Cir. 2021), *cert. granted sub nom.* Nation v. Brackeen, 142 S. Ct. 1204, 212 L. Ed. 2d 215 (2022), and *cert. granted*, 142 S. Ct. 1205, 212 L. Ed. 2d 215 (2022), and *cert. granted sub nom.* Texas v. Haaland, 142 S. Ct. 1205, 212 L. Ed. 2d 215 (2022), and *cert. granted*, 142 S. Ct. 1205, 212 L. Ed. 2d 215 (2022).

# Index